COLIN LANKSHEAR is a Mexican Council for Science and Technology Heritage Fellow based in the Center for University Studies at the National Autonomous University of Mexico. He is author of *Changing Literacies* (Open University Press 1997), *The New Work Order* (with James Paul Gee and Glynda Hull, Allen & Unwin and Westview 1996) and *Literacy, Schooling and Revolution* (Falmer 1987, 1989).

ILANA SNYDER teaches in the Faculty of Education at Monash University and is author of *Hypertext* (Melbourne University Press and New York University Press 1997) and editor of *Page to Screen* (Allen & Unwin and Routledge 1997).

BILL GREEN is Professor of Curriculum Studies at the University of New England. He is editor of *The Insistence of the Letter* (Falmer 1993), *Teaching the English Subjects* (Deakin University Press 1996) and *Designs on Learning* (ACSA 1999).

Teachers and Technoliteracy

Managing literacy, technology and learning in schools

Colin Lankshear and Ilana Snyder
with Bill Green

ALLEN & UNWIN

First published in 2000 by
Allen & Unwin
9 Atchison Street
St Leonards NSW 1590
Australia
Phone: (61 2) 8425 0100
Fax: (61 2) 9906 2218
Email: frontdesk@allen-unwin.com.au
Web: http://www.allen-unwin.com.au

National Library of Australia
Cataloguing-in-Publication entry:

Lankshear, Colin.
  Teachers and technoliteracy: managing literacy,
  technology and learning in schools.

  Bibliography.
  Includes index.
  ISBN 1 86448 946 4.

  1. Technological literacy. 2. Computers and literacy.
  3. Computer-assisted instruction. 4. Educational technology.
  5. Literacy—Social aspects. 6. Information technology.
  I. Green, Bill. II. Snyder, Ilana, 1949– . III. Title.

371.334

Set in 10.5/12 pt Weiss by DOCUPRO, Sydney
Printed by SRM Production Services Sdn Bhd, Malaysia

This book draws directly on the research project, *Digital Rhetorics: Literacies and Technologies in Education—Current Practices and Future Directions*. The members of the research team were: Colin Lankshear, Chris Bigum, Cal Durrant, Bill Green, Eileen Honan, Wendy Morgan, Joy Murray, Ilana Snyder and Martyn Wild. The project was funded by the Department of Employment, Education, Training and Youth Affairs, through the Children's Literacy National Projects Program.

Contents

.

A note on authorship

This book has grown out of a research project funded by the Department of Employment, Education, Training and Youth Affairs (DEETYA) through the Children's Literacy National Projects Program. The research was reported as *Digital Rhetorics: Literacies and Technologies in Education—Current Practices and Future Directions* (Lankshear et al. 1997). The original project was undertaken by a consortium of researchers jointly led by Colin Lankshear (then located at Queensland University of Technology) and Chris Bigum (Central Queensland University). Ilana Snyder (Monash University) and Bill Green (University of New England) were members of this consortium. Other members were Cal Durrant (University of New England), Eileen Honan (Queensland University of Technology), Wendy Morgan (Queensland University of Technology), Joy Murray (New South Wales Department of Education & Training) and Martyn Wild (Edith Cowan University). In addition, Robert Bleicher, Michele Knobel and Ann McKenna were closely involved in the case study and final report write-ups. Researchers working in the several sites enjoyed admirable research assistance from David Baxter, Belinda Easthead, Paul Muirhead, Steve Roffe, Francy Ross and Colin Warren.

While this book draws considerably on the contributions of all the participants named here, it could not have been written by such a large group. From the outset, the consortium envisaged various productions based on the research by combinations of writers as time, individual energies and competing commitments allowed. This book varies significantly in focus, orientation and emphasis from the project report, which was slanted heavily in the direction of being able to make finite and succinct recommendations to DEETYA, state education departments, teacher education providers and schools. Our emphasis here varies from *Digital Rhetorics* in two main ways. First, it aims to speak in a sustained manner to practitioners about how to go about 'doing' literacy and technology in schools. The school studies, policy analysis and theoretical insights are interconnected and cross-referenced in a form that we hope is easy to navigate and has clear meaning and application for busy teachers coping with the pressures and demands of day-to-day life in schools. This is a significant shift in specific focus, orientation and audience from the original report. Second, it reflects the personal emphases, styles and values of the present authors in ways that are not necessarily shared by all of the research participants.

Initially this book was to be written jointly by Colin Lankshear, Ilana Snyder and Bill Green. During the writing period, however, Bill's schedules and commitments limited his active writing role. He made available to us, in the best collegial manner, texts he had written that were germane to our shared vision for the book. He also read the manuscript, commenting as time permitted. Readers familiar with Bill's work will appreciate just how vividly his ideas and perspectives are present in this book. In the end, Bill decided, in his characteristically principled way, to resist our wishes to have him named as a full, joint author. We regretfully accepted Bill's decision, but at the same time want to acknowledge fully the depth and extent of his considerable intellectual contribution, for which we are most grateful.

We also want to mention the contributions to the original report of Chris Bigum and Jane Kenway, Cal Durrant and Joy Murray, Eileen Honan, Robert Bleicher, Michele Knobel and Richard Smith, who will see a good deal of their efforts reflected in these pages.

In the end, while much of the credit for whatever may be of value in this book belongs to our colleagues, we alone assume responsibility for any shortcomings.

Colin Lankshear, Mexico City
Ilana Snyder, Melbourne

Acknowledgments

In addition to those people whose contributions to this book are acknowledged in the note on authorship, we would like to thank others who participated in the project on which our work is based.

The original research project on literacies and technologies in education was funded by the Commonwealth Department of Employment, Education, Training and Youth Affairs (DEETYA) through the Children's Literacy National Project. The views expressed in this book, however, like those in the original report, do not necessarily represent the views of what is now known as the Commonwealth Department of Education, Training and Youth Affairs (DETYA).

We owe thanks to members of the advisory committee for the original research project. Our committee served us admirably, providing good advice and feedback, and the efforts of its members are much appreciated. The members were: Mike Berry, Paul Brock (to July 1996), Stephanie Gunn, Claire Houston, Kaye Lowe, Marion Meiers, David Potter, Michael Ryan, Richard Smith, Lee Willett and Anna Zantiotis.

We would also like to pay special tribute to the classroom teachers and students whose generosity and goodwill made the site studies possible. They are the people to whom this book is dedicated. We wish them success and satisfaction in their future lives and work, and may they go from strength to strength.

We thank the principals of the schools involved in the original study and those state department personnel in New South Wales, Queensland and Victoria who in various ways actively supported and facilitated the school-based studies.

For permission to reproduce diagrams, we thank the International Reading Association and Blackwell.

Finally, we thank Elizabeth Weiss of Allen & Unwin for believing in the potential of the original study and our ability to build on it in ways that might justify a wider readership than the original report could hope to reach.

Preface

This book is about how to 'do' literacy and technology in educationally effective ways, in classrooms, in countries like Australia, Britain, Canada, New Zealand and the United States. We do not suggest that teachers and schools must integrate new technologies into classroom work; at the same time, we recognise that resisting the pressure to take up technology is becoming more difficult by the day.

We believe, rather, that there are vital educational purposes and standards that must not be sacrificed to the technological dance or to the escalating corporatisation of education with which new technologies are so closely associated. If and where teachers and schools decide that they will integrate new communication and information technologies into curriculum and pedagogy, it is crucial that they keep these educational purposes and standards clearly in focus.

Right now, teachers are under enormous pressure to technologise learning. Similarly, individuals, families, businesses and institutions are made to feel that they are not keeping up if they have not wired their world to the web and linked their labours to a Local Area Network (LAN). While it is true that anyone who avoids, or is denied access to, acquiring facility with new technologies may be marginalised in the world beyond schools, nothing hard and fast follows as far as computers in classrooms are concerned. The fact that owning and driving a car is regarded as the norm for 'our way of life' has not led to driving instruction becoming a part of the school curriculum. Any number of people—including one of the authors of this book—have opted for lifestyles in which owning and driving a car has no place and even makes little sense. What is more, the fact that mainstream life is becoming increasingly 'technologised' is not a necessary thing, let alone a good thing. From such perspectives we might well resent the almost inescapable coercion schools face with respect to taking up new technologies.

Yet, if there is something constructive to say about the intense pressure schools find themselves under to technologise learning, it is that it provokes anew important questions: What does educating young people require of us? What priorities do we have to recommit to, and preserve, as we set about educating under a new technological regimen? What, if anything, comes with the adoption of new technologies that might require us to pay close attention to the purposes of education? We cannot take these questions too seriously. Unfortunately, the incursion of new technologies into our educational lives coincides, by no means accidentally, with other things. These include an intensification of teachers' work, concerted attacks on teachers' conditions, and the openness with which interested groups conspire to undermine confidence in public schools by manufacturing successive 'crises' in school performance.

Currently, we are witnesses to a broad-based assault on schools which is designed to lay the ground for corporatising education and opening it up as a new frontier for business activity and entrepreneurship. Teachers should be in no doubt that their profession and occupations are under attack by unfriendly forces. Moreover, they need to be aware of the extent to which the push to technologise education is intimately tied up with interests most eager to undermine the tradition of public education.

In an important book, *No More Teachers, No More Books: The Commercialization of Canada's Schools*, Heather-jane Robertson (1998) amasses chilling evidence of the nexus between the computing industry, mass media, the corporate business world, supernational neoliberal organisations like the OECD, and neoliberal politicians, bureaucrats and 'advisers'. In concert, these interest groups are determined to give schooling a commercial 'make-over' and open it up to privatised provision. In the short run, this involves turning schools into renewed 'ideology machines' to promote the development of economically motivated, self-interested individuals. In the long run, it involves turning public schools into distant memories, in a world in which learning becomes a Microsoft-style 'anytime, anywhere' engagement. In the medium term, it means exposing schools to corporate influence and commercial activity—education for profit.

To set the scene for what we say in this book, it is useful to consider briefly the wider context in which curriculum and pedagogy are being technologised. We also need to keep in mind that trends that are rapidly becoming the norm in some countries may be less apparent in our own contexts but, nonetheless, well on the way.

Robertson (1998: 30) cites a ministry of education official in a Canadian province, who said: 'I think there are two essentials for kindergarten. The first is to get them ready for keyboarding. The other is to get these little kids to start thinking of themselves as "Me, Inc"'. In a similar vein, a high-profile North American education summit, set up in 1995 and co-hosted by IBM's chief executive officer, Louis V. Gerstner, focused on 'the need for world class academic standards . . . [to] provide an opportunity for governors and business leaders to understand and experience how emerging technologies can be incorporated into school restructuring' (cited in Robertson 1998: 34).

In a 1997 paper published in the *Electronic School*, 'Are corporate technology initiatives more PR than philanthropy?', Karen Southwick quotes the president of the IBM Foundation, Stanley Litow, who acknowledges that 'our strategic focus has been to figure out the ways you can use technology to systematically fix the flaws in the school system. We decided to treat education as if it were a very important and sophisticated business problem' (cited in Robertson 1998: 132). Robertson reports that by the early 1980s key participants in the New America Schools Development Corporation (NASDC) like AT&T, IBM and the American Stock Exchange had supported corporate-friendly school-reform projects to the tune of millions of dollars. In short, Robertson (1998: 161) concludes:

> Technology has been sold as an enlightened, inexpensive, and surprise-free tool that can lift students to personal excellence, moral certitude, and international competitiveness at the same time. The promise has all the credibility of a time-share brochure, and much of it is written in the same language.

This is a language that happily equates 'data' with 'information', and 'information' with 'knowledge' and 'understanding', making it that much easier to redesign education around information retrieval. Yet teachers have always known that an important responsibility of education is to help learners understand how one moves from information to knowledge, and how to make critical judgments about the quality of information. One of the notable trends observed in the 'Digital Rhetorics' project—which provides the stimulus and resource for this book and which we revisit in later chapters—is the gap between recognising the distinctions between 'getting information' and 'assessing information' on the one hand, and 'seeking information' and 'coming to know something' on the other (Lankshear et al. 1997). The challenge for teachers is to build these distinctions into computer-mediated classroom work Failure to enact such distinctions plays directly into the hands of those who would reduce education to information pursuit and retrieval, and who would sell us the 'gadgets' to realise this dimunition of a key responsibility. Teachers do well to recall Theodore Roszak's (1996) observation that people who think 'education' and the 'pursuit of information' are synonymous have no understanding of either.

By the same token, the cautions we are sounding are not intended to establish a blanket case against the educational use of new technologies in schools. Not at all. We are in favour of pedagogical approaches and supporting technologies that serve educational ends and promote educational outcomes equitably and effectively, as well as efficiently. In Neil Postman's words, we are 'not arguing against using computers in schools . . . [We are] arguing against our sleepwalking attitudes toward it, against allowing it to distract us from important things, against making a god of it' (Postman 1996: 207).

In other words, we are not technology 'boosters' (Bigum & Kenway 1998), fixed on contributing to the hard sell of communication and information technologies to schools. We believe that teachers need to approach the technologising of literacy and curriculum with caution, understanding and wisdom. As we argue in a later chapter, we need to ensure that 'education remains the main game' and that technologies, new or old, remain faithfully in the service of that main game.

This book is written for teachers who find themselves committing, or are already committed, to the integration of new technologies into learning, but who are searching for ways to ensure that this integration serves educational ends. It is written for teachers who want to do all they can to ensure that their profession is not reduced to the status of a servant to the corporate world, to the military–industrial complex, or to a neoliberal ethos dedicated to policy directions that have spurred the dramatic growth of the gap between rich and poor. It is for teachers who believe that literacy is more than the capacity to encode and decode—to grasp meanings inscribed on a page or a screen, or within an established social practice. It is for teachers who believe that being literate also involves the capacity and disposition to scrutinise the practices and universes of meanings within which texts are embedded. It is for teachers who believe that being literate entails the capability to enter actively into creating, shaping and transforming social practices and universes of meanings in search of the best and most humane of all possible worlds.

In opposition to reductionist and mechanistic views of literacy and learning, we argue that education must enable learners to become proficient with what we call the 'operational', 'cultural' and 'critical' dimensions of literacy and technology. We explain what we mean by these three dimensions and how they might be useful in providing teachers with a framework within which to think about the day-to-day demands and challenges associated with the use of the new technologies in classrooms.

Becoming proficient with the 'operational', 'cultural' and 'critical' dimensions includes understanding how contemporary economic, social, technological, administrative, organisational and political changes are affecting the social practices of literacy, technology and learning. It also includes understanding how these changes are altering literacy, technology and learning and the relationships among them. Further, it incorporates understanding how current changes are placing new 'premiums' on literacy, technology and learning—raising them to new heights of urgency. Most importantly, becoming adept with the 'operational', 'cultural' and 'critical' dimensions suggests ways in which teachers may be able to respond effectively to the new demands associated with technology use.

Our aim is to speak directly to teachers about the practical aspects of taking on literacy and new technologies in schools. Doing this, however, involves more than simply taking account of practical matters. It requires the support of useful ideas and evidence from research and theory, as well as reference to the larger context within which classroom practice takes place. We connect and cross-reference school studies, policy analysis and theoretical insights in ways that teachers should find meaningful amid the everyday demands of school life. We draw on the experiences of real teachers and offer suggestions about how to pursue effective learning practices in classrooms under conditions that are often difficult.

The book is informed by emerging theories of literacy, technology and learning that we attempt to make explicit and accessible. The fact that the theories are developing should be seen not as a weakness, rather as an appropriate, even inevitable, response to the rapidly changing, dynamic qualities of new information and communication technologies and the new literacy practices associated with their use. In the age of the internet, we need to formulate theories that are as dynamic as the technologies themselves, but that are also critical and reflexive. These theories need to be responsive to the rapidly changing conditions that now govern the world. The theories we present and discuss are evolving: they are theories in the making.

This book is also informed by the activities and efforts of real teachers and students in real classrooms. We present stories of teachers, students, learning, technology and change. Each story is unique, but together they demonstrate a number of patterns that have helped in identifying a set of educational principles intended to guide the integration of new technologies into classroom teaching and learning. The identification and explanation of these patterns and principles, built on important and illuminating work by Chris Bigum and Jane Kenway (1998), is a key component of the book, and underlies the practical suggestions we advance in the final chapter.

We hope this book will be of interest and value to literacy teachers first and foremost, but also to several other groups: teachers in different subject areas, who remain concerned with the literacy needs of their students when new technologies are used; school administrators interested in educational change; academics and students focused on literacy, technology and learning issues; and people more broadly concerned with educational theory, policy and reform. We have tried to present our arguments in a way that will be relevant and useful to all these groups. The proof of this, one way or the other, must lie in the reading.

Before we begin the main text, a final point needs to be mentioned. *Teachers and Technoliteracy* is informed by teachers and students who took us into their classrooms in good faith and with much trust. Such a research situation creates opportunities that have the potential to contribute to the enhancement of educational practice. It also generates certain risks. Foremost among these is the risk of demeaning or slighting classroom work.

Our explicit purpose of identifying ways to enhance practice involves identifying not only instances where we think things have been done well, from which we can learn, but also instances where we think things could have been done better, from which we can also learn. There is no point in researchers undertaking this kind of work if they cannot and do not identify limitations as well as strengths. The point, however, is always to do such work constructively, sensitively and respectfully. And this we have endeavoured to do.

Where necessary, we have disguised examples superficially, while trying to preserve the features relevant to the issues we wish to raise. As one of our colleagues from the 'Digital Rhetorics' project reminded us: 'Teachers are committed people, who spend all their time and energy devising new and exciting ways for their kids to learn. But, like the rest of us, they're learning too and this is where they've reached in their own journey right now'. Indeed, many of the teachers whose classrooms we observed had reached their points in the journey under highly 'unpropitious' conditions. This needs to be acknowledged.

Where we focus on what we think are limitations in classroom work, we do so in full recognition that these are not reflections of personal shortcomings of teachers and learners. Rather, they go to the heart of important issues that include: the conditions under which teachers learn to be teachers; policy directions and directives; resourcing decisions; and administrative and political agendas. These agendas construe 'devolution' in terms of concentrating power and decision-making at the centre, and pushing down to teachers at the front line the responsibility for working miracles on shrinking budgets. Moreover, these agendas are being implemented in the face of social, economic and demographic conditions: 'schools have never had to deal with so many students who couldn't care less, and who have so little reason to care more' (Robertson 1998: 32).

Just as we tried to carry out the research constructively, sensitively and respectfully, we have strived to write up the descriptions of the schools and classrooms with care. Where we fail, we apologise. Where we succeed, it is no more than the due of the exemplary teachers who accepted us unconditionally into their classrooms. In every instance, we had the privilege of watching these teachers offer everything they had, with enthusiasm and a passion for the welfare of their students. We hope that some of the things we say will speak to these teachers and their colleagues in ways that will help them work the miracles they are called on daily to achieve.

PLAN OF THE BOOK

Chapter 1 gives a taste of our school-based research and identifies some issues and themes emerging from portraits of three schools. Such portraits, and the issues and themes they stimulate, give at least a preliminary sense of the challenges that face literacy teachers at present in the context of current technological change. These issues and themes are developed and enlarged, and additional ones are introduced, in the chapters that follow.

In chapter 2 we look more closely at literacy, technology and learning in ways that help us understand current practices and anticipate future directions for classroom work involving new technologies. We begin by examining literacy, technology and learning, then consider how we might move toward an integrated view of all three constructs.

In chapter 3 we look at the policy dimension of teachers' work. As education is now very much a policy-driven sector, teachers cannot escape engaging with policy. We identify the main functions of policy and the key policy roles teachers need to play in their professional lives. Next, we briefly describe a selection of national and state-level policy documents that apply directly to the interface between technology, literacy and learning. We then consider their implications for developing policies helpful in translating curriculum and syllabus requirements into effective classroom programs. The chapter concludes with an example of teacher policy development that exemplifies many of the qualities and procedures we believe make for the creation of useful school-level policies covering literacy, technology and learning across the curriculum.

Chapter 4 adds to the picture of current practices sketched in the portraits presented in chapter 1. In studies from further sites and classrooms, key features are identified, added to those of the three portraits in chapter 1, and brought together as a summary statement of what the site studies have collectively told us about current classroom learning practices involving literacies and new technologies. These studies provide an information base from which to develop ideas, strategies and plans for building on existing strengths and addressing current shortcomings in pedagogy, policy and professional understanding at the literacy–technology interface.

In chapter 5 we advance a framework of patterns and principles we believe are useful for thinking about what we have found. These patterns and principles provide a basis for developing systematic, coherent and informed approaches to furthering literacy education in an age where information and communication practices are increasingly mediated by information and communication technologies.

Chapter 6 translates this framework into concrete suggestions, recommendations and guidelines designed to assist those whose job it is to provide a sound literacy education in the so-called 'information age'.

1

Literacies, technologies and classrooms

This book is about a new era in literacy education. In a world increasingly mediated by communication and information technologies, teachers are faced with far-reaching demands to integrate the new technologies into teaching and learning. These demands leave many teachers feeling overwhelmed and confused. We are not 'technophiles' ourselves, but we believe that schools probably cannot avoid the massive incursions of new technologies into all facets of life. New technologies have radically altered our everyday modes of communication. They are becoming so fundamental to our society that most areas of social practice in day-to-day life are affected by the so-called 'information revolution'.

Much has been written and said about the information revolution, with varying degrees of clarity. Discussions of the impact of the new technologies are often clouded by hype. Enthusiasts openly embrace the technologies, claiming they offer a panacea for educational problems, enhance communication, empower users and democratise classrooms. At the opposite extreme, 'demonisers' exude cynicism about the technologies' apparent powers. Some dismiss them as simply new instructional and communication tools. Others reject them outright as yet a further form of social control or enforced consumption, which promotes the interests of state and corporate sectors. Unfortunately, extreme responses are of limited use, and the need to move beyond them is increasingly urgent in education. Cutting through the hype is essential, as it is too often associated with a hard sell and wastage of valuable resources.

Rather than adopting either a booster or a 'luddite' position, the challenge for teachers is to learn how to approach the use of the new technologies efficiently, ethically and responsibly, with a view to tapping their educational potential. To avoid getting swept up in the faddish character of much that is happening in schools or just 'going along for the ride', teachers need to develop and build on critically informed perspectives laced with a shot of healthy scepticism. At the same time, there is no point in trying to accommodate new technologies to existing classroom approaches, as such teaching ends up looking much the way it always has—except that it is more 'technologised'. We believe that, if they are approached sensitively and sensibly, new technologies offer teachers expansive possibilities for innovation and professional renewal, as well as important new possibilities for learning.

To meet the emerging educational challenge presented by new technologies, teachers need to be able to base their judgments of the potential of new technologies for classroom teaching and learning on real experience and informed personal understanding. They need to find effective and appropriate ways of using these technologies to help prepare students to participate independently, competently and critically in post-school contexts.

We hasten to point out that it is not necessary for teachers to become confident users before thinking about how to apply communication and information technologies in the classroom. Indeed, learning how to use the technologies and thinking about ways to integrate them into the curriculum are symbiotic processes that develop best concurrently rather than in a linear progression, one proscribed till the other is achieved.

This book draws on a combination of recent research into experiences of teachers and learners in Australian classrooms, as well as on a wider body of theory, policy and research, in an attempt to inform efforts by teachers, schools and administration to tackle the challenge we have identified.

KEY QUESTIONS

A number of questions immediately arise with respect to the challenge teachers in general and literacy teachers in particular face around the role and significance of new technologies in school education. These include: Guided Q :

- How may literacy teachers learn to use new technologies effectively in their professional work?
- What pedagogical models exist that take literacy and technology into account in ways on which teachers can build for classroom use?
- How are literacy and technology related, and how can literacy teachers make sense of this relationship to develop sound pedagogy?
- What do national, state and school-based policies say about integrating new technologies into classroom literacy practices that is relevant to literacy teachers?
- What experiences, research literature and theory are available that can inform policy, curriculum and classroom practices in useful ways?
- What sorts of principles exist for guiding the integration of new technologies into classroom learning?
- What methods count as sound uses of new technologies in classroom-based literacy education?

These and similar questions are at the heart of this book, which is especially concerned with trying to explain how an understanding of the complex relationships between literacy and technology can be translated into workable pedagogical practices.

BACK TO THE SOURCE

A good way of situating our subject matter and getting a fix on the nature of the challenge facing teachers is to go 'back to the source'—to take a look inside some real classrooms in real Australian schools. We begin our discussion by offering portraits of classroom work using new technologies in three quite different schools. These sketches try to capture how teachers are approaching the use of new information and communication technologies for literacy purposes. The first is a geographically remote school; the second is a well-resourced private school in a large city; the third is a small, multicultural primary school, also located in a large city. The stories of these teachers and their students illuminate the contrasting ways in which they have confronted the challenges associated with integrating the use of new technologies into curriculum practices. Each portrait looks at the kind of 'culture' the schools and classrooms are trying to build around the use of new technologies; the sorts of policies, if any, they have developed to guide the integration of new technologies into school life; and examples of classroom pedagogy.

The sketches are based on brief, but intensive and highly focused, investigations of the three classrooms. These were just three of twenty teachers and their classrooms, from eleven research sites, in three Australian states, that agreed to participate in a national project (Lankshear et al. 1997). Other sites are described later in the book. We wanted to witness, 'capture' and describe a range of illuminating instances of practice using new technologies in literacy education: looking for telling cases, so to speak. In most cases, data were collected over just three or four days. These data included contextual or background information; artefacts (for example, policy documents and statements, lists of technology resources, descriptions of student work); audiotapes and transcripts of interviews; and observation notes. Our emphasis was on finding and describing illustrative instances of practice—particular events or episodes that were likely to be similar to other events and episodes, both at that site and at others. The focus of the analysis and interpretation of the data was on what the descriptions could tell us about how to achieve the kinds of practices and outcomes we believe schools should be seeking.

Consequently, our investigations in no way pretend to be exhaustive of all that went on. Neither do the portraits claim to be representative of practice as a whole in these sites—still less of schools at large. We describe practices as we saw them to illustrate significant points about literacy, technology and learning. This is not the same thing as assigning an essence to what we observed, and it is certainly not to imply that what we did not see in particular instances did not go on elsewhere. The portraits of classroom activities are used simply for illustrative purposes. The ideas emerging from classroom portraits can then be linked to larger patterns and principles, which are intended to enhance future practice on a more extensive scale.

In no way are we telling these stories to criticise teacher performance, curriculum content and school policy. This important point should be borne in mind at all times when reading the book. Our purpose is to learn from real instances of real practices to better understand the challenges presented to education by the rapid introduction of new technologies into classrooms, and how to take account of these challenges. Teachers did not seek this additional challenge to an already taxing job. They inherited it by default. Our job is to see what can be learned from attempts to meet this challenge, to suggest how we might all set about tackling it as effectively as possible, to share the load equitably and to distribute responsibilities fairly.

Caldwell Primary School

Caldwell Primary is a prep to Year 6 school in a small, agricultural community. It has 25 students and two teaching staff. The teacher-principal, Ron, was appointed in 1989. He sensed at that time the growing importance of technology in school education. The school, however, had only one Apple IIe computer. Ron did a short computer course and was inspired by what he envisaged might be done with computers in primary classrooms.

In 1991 the school purchased its first Macintosh, mainly for word-processing. During his career Ron had seen many students disheartened by having to redraft their work. He thought the simple fact that word-processing eliminates recopying might provide an incentive for such students to write more and perhaps to revise their texts. Keen to provide the infant school with a writing laboratory, Ron purchased a Digi-Card system from a high school and began collecting and linking discarded Apple IIes. When the state Department of Education funding model shifted to individual school discretion in the late 1980s, Ron seized the opportunity to upgrade the school's technology resources.

At first, parents were reluctant to support the push for technology. Reasons included: 'We don't want our kids any smarter than we are!', and 'They'll never learn how to write by hand'. Undeterred, Ron engaged the students in computer-mediated activities at school until they began pressuring their parents to buy computers for use at home. Since 1991 Ron has spent more than $20 000 on information technology resources. Currently the school has more than twenty computers, one with CD-ROM, another with modem and internet access, although eleven are Apple IIes, dating back to the early 1980s. There are six printers. The equipment is located in the staff room, the classrooms and the enclosed verandah. Overall, the student–computer ratio is almost one to one.

Originally, the computers in the enclosed verandah space

had been in a demountable building, adjacent to the staff room, that was used as a library. Students had access to these facilities during lunchtime and recess, as they could be seen from the staff room. Just when these computers were about to be networked, the school was downgraded to a 'two-building school' because of falling numbers. The demountable library was removed and its contents stored wherever possible. The loss of the library demoralised the school. The PCs were put on desks in a space with insufficient power points to operate them and which exposed them to damage from heat and rodents. Students were denied access to the computers during lunch and recess because they could no longer be supervised. Facing a dispersed and rapidly deteriorating library collection and the inconvenient relocation of computers, Ron applied for a Department of Education grant to build a room, a library and a technology centre. The money was approved, provided the school raised an equal amount. This was achieved by means of the Parents and Citizens Association, additional community support, and by redirecting funds from the school's operating budget.

Although Caldwell does not have a technology and literacy policy (there does not seem to be time or need to produce a formal document), its emphasis on technology is strong, not least because of the principal's commitment. Ron makes resourcing and curriculum decisions and takes responsibility for keeping on top of IT developments and promoting literacy and technology from the school budget. He seeks advice about software and hardware purchasing decisions from informed local residents, commercial catalogues or demonstrations by salespeople. A newly appointed regional consultant helped Ron to network some existing equipment and to maximise student access to the internet with the single, modem-connected computer. Given the school's isolation, Ron encouraged staff participation in the state education department's program to improve the teaching and learning of technology. While some aspects of the program were useful, the advances Caldwell can make using the internet are limited by its unreliable internet connection.

While talk of 'basic skills' and 'literacy levels' is common at Caldwell, the school has not assigned technology the role of ensuring success in these areas. Rather than let technology become an engine driving the curriculum, efforts have been made to integrate technology into appropriate curriculum and pedagogy. There is obvious enthusiasm for learning activities at Caldwell and a strong sense of what schooling means for students' futures. Teachers combine structured teaching tasks and group and individual work to promote transfer of peer knowledge and skills. Classroom observations, like the following, capture the prevailing approach to pedagogy at the school:

> Carol ushers the students into the classroom and directs those who wish to listen to her read Lockie Leonard, Human Torpedo (Winton 1993) to sit on the floor or at their desks. Seven students choose to listen, while three students move to the back of the room where they settle down in front of their computers. Another three go out on to the verandah, where the Macs are located.
>
> One of these students, a Year 4 girl, quickly opens a ClarisWorks painting file. She is planning to do some illustrations for a friend's Christmas card. Two other children have paired up at a computer and are engaged in using Treasure Maths. Inside the classroom, a Year 4 boy is engrossed in the story he is writing. He says he produces a one-page story every second day on an Apple IIe using Magic Slate II. Another girl in Year 3 is constructing a Christmas card using ClarisWorks. She is competent at importing and reformatting graphics, ClipArt or text.
>
> A third student, a Year 5 boy, is also working at one of the computers, shaping a narrative. Ron tells us that before arriving at Caldwell this boy scored poorly on the basic skills test, but under Ron's charge he has become immersed in the use of computers and is now writing stories of one page or more every day. Since the removal of the library building, Carol, a casual teacher who relieves the principal one day a week and works with the Year 3–6 class, has become adept at using encyclopaedia software. The students like to use the CD-ROM facilities for getting information, but there is no alternative, as the print encyclopaedias have been unavailable since the library building was removed.

Our classroom observations revealed students working on individual projects and stories most of the class time. One computer per student allowed for extended use of the technology and released the teachers for individual conferencing and tuition. In the main, each teacher's time was spent as facilitator, friend and guide.

Like their teachers, the students see technology skills as integral to their future. Erin believes she will be doing 'everything on computers' when she grows up, and that everyone will own one. Gary says that he uses the new technologies 'all the time . . . every day'. Both students believe that they can become more effective operators of technology in their schooling. Asked if she liked using computers, Erin responded that she does now, but 'once they were my worst enemy'. Pressed about how she might improve her efficiency, she suggested having a specialist sit with her for extended periods of time. By contrast, Gary sometimes does his homework and stories on the family's home-based IBM-compatible; he also plays games for up to two hours a week. The students interviewed believed that they probably have more access to technology at Caldwell than most Australian school children.

Many of the students at Caldwell have managerial aspirations, either in the town or on neighbouring farms, and recognise the need to become familiar with the new technologies. Ron and Carol believe that the students will be unemployable unless they are computer-literate. Ron says that as 50 per cent of the students from Caldwell proceed to university they need IT skills. A major frustration at Caldwell is that they have the hardware to use the internet in the potentially exciting ways they discovered in the state education department's program to improve the teaching and learning of technology, but the shortcomings of the phone lines prevent them from doing so.

When the library building existed, Caldwell might well have been the envy of the vast majority of rural schools. This has changed. There is little out-of-class access available now because of the supervision problems created by the new location of the hardware, but there is another explanation. Ron admits that, despite his push for technology, he has resisted allowing children open access to the computers at lunchtime because, given the opportunity, students will concentrate so much on technology that they will lose interest in playing sport. As the school has demonstrated swimming and athletic prowess in the past, Ron is careful not to place this tradition in jeopardy by allowing the district's sporting record to dissipate. For Ron this is a strategic decision. If the community perceived that the school's sporting performance was dropping because of technology, his work in persuading the community that technology was worth pursuing might be undone.

Ealing Grammar

Ealing Grammar is a private girls' school (P–12) in a major capital city. We begin this portrait of the school's approach to literacy, technology and learning with snapshots of two English classes that were participating in the Year 7 'Multimedia' project. The students were required to produce a HyperCard stack, designed like an interactive story, on a modern myth or legend. They were encouraged to use their imagination in writing, graphics, promoting interactivity and effective design, all directed at producing an entertaining story. The emphasis in the project was on providing opportunities for the students to be creative, not on acquiring skills in the use of multimedia technology.

Class one

The students are all working individually at their computers. There is a high level of engagement and concentration; no-one moves around the room. The sounds are mainly computer-generated: the click of the mouse, the clatter of keyboards, the noises from activated sound cards. There is no freewheeling. The students are focused on producing their multimedia versions of a myth. They are motivated, involved and focused. There is little interaction.

The Computer Awareness teacher moves from student to student as consultant, or troubleshooter. When students want her help they raise their hands and wait patiently till she comes over. She is an important resource; her manner is confident and she responds quickly to student queries. She uses the language of technology and it seems to be a shared language.

The teacher is on the go the entire lesson, always watching for students who need help. She is both confident and competent with the technology. She explains to a student how to create a folder in which the stack will be located. She takes a piece of paper to sketch the folder and what it contains: she 'represents' what she is explaining. She talks to the student, but also listens to her. As she explains about the folder, two other girls have their hands raised. The teacher makes a mental note that these students require her help. She doesn't get flustered, but she also does not suggest that they consult their peers.

Class two

There is no formal beginning to the lesson. The students walk in, switch on their computers and get right into the Multimedia task. The technical assistant asks early on whether there are any problems. One student wants to know how to create an icon and a friend shows her the procedure. Except for this request, the kinds of questions raised here are different. They are not about technical matters but seem to be more English-related—about the text and how to develop it effectively. The students in this class are more interactive than in the first. They talk to each other about their evolving texts. But when asked to be quiet, as a group is ready to record sound, there is immediate silence.

The atmosphere in this class is more relaxed. Some of the talk is dedicated to a discussion of the different media required to create the stories. It seems that the students in this group completed a draft of the story before they began creating the multimedia environment. The girls stare at their screens. Their eyes are focused as their hands work the mouse. The screen has a strange drawing power, as if it is a magnet. It seems that we can almost 'see' them thinking.

These are typical snapshots of how new technologies are used at Ealing for literacy purposes: something which has been on Ealing's agenda since the first microcomputers appeared in schools in the late 1970s. Those in leadership roles claim to take great care to ensure that technology does not drive the curriculum. While technologies are seen as integral to the school culture and fabric, Ealing is not a 'technology school' and does not promote itself in terms of its technology program.

Changes in practices involving new technologies are based on inclusive consultation. Top-down imposition of technology policies is avoided. Teachers have ample opportunities and encouragement to plan and prepare for changes to their professional practices. At Ealing, teachers employ an informal yet effective approach for learning about the role of new technologies within the school environment. They find someone who can do what they want to understand and learn how to do it from them. Conscious efforts are made to develop a 'learning community' which allows change to happen.

Ealing's overarching technology objective is to equip all students by Year 10 with a comprehensive range of computer skills and competencies, and familiarity with a number of computer applications. Ealing intends that by their final year of study each student will possess a 'software toolkit' and the ability to apply the skills purposefully. The 'basic toolkit' includes: word processing; spreadsheeting; graphic design and drawing; desktop publishing; multimedia presentation; multimedia authoring; internet researching; and internet communications. The 'super toolkit' includes: scanning; printing; using CD-ROMs for re-search; internet accessing; using digital photography; sound and video recording and editing.

The Year 7 project we observed is part of this greater plan for computer integration within the curriculum. This cross-curriculum project involves students creating multimedia texts in Art, History, Geography and English. Teachers prepare in advance for their roles in the project. They attend professional development sessions at the school to learn how to use the technologies. Additional technological support is available in the computer labs when teachers and students work on the project.

The school is well endowed with infrastructure. In some rooms, class sets of laptops are available. Internet access is available in the library and several other locations. There are eight computers in the staff room that are in constant use. The main locus for computer activity, however, is the labs. In 1994 the school entered a partnership with Optus Vision to trial the Optus high-speed, broadband connection to the internet. A separate LAN was installed in the library, comprising twelve computers for student use and two computers in the library-staff work area. Subsequent extensions to this network allow more than 150 simultaneous connections to the internet. Previously, the three available connections had been in the staff room, the library and the curriculum coordinator's office. When the Optus project was initiated, the head of IT and Computing gave presentations at school assemblies, projecting the computer display onto a large screen and demonstrating what could be done using the internet. A subsequent session on the web, conducted by the librarians, introduced all classes from 7–12 to the internet.

The Optus project stimulated extended staff discussion, and consideration of the curriculum and pedagogical implications of using the web. Staff discussed a wide range of issues: the structure of schooling; critical literacy; the internet as a research resource; support, training and ethics. One librarian took a further initiative: to work closely with teachers across the cur-riculum to encourage the use of the internet with students.

While there is no single document articulating Ealing's technology policy, the key to the school's approach is clear. Curriculum initiatives are ever-evolving and rely on a strong, supportive culture, involving all students and teachers with access to technology when required and subject–teacher involvement at all levels.

At Ealing, the push for development of dexterity with technology has come mostly from the computer teachers and specialists. Of late, the English teachers as a group are beginning to consider the implications for literacy practices. They have also, however, been among the most reluctant 'uptakers', expressing concern about the extra demands put on an already crammed English curriculum. They felt the Multimedia project would take time away from what they saw as the real business of English—writing, and the study of printed texts. To tackle this issue, it was planned that the English teachers would participate in a project using hypertext webs. The emphasis would be on developing texts, but texts with links. 'Hypertext has great significance for the teaching of English', argued the head of IT. Part of the challenge was to convince the teachers of this.

The head of IT, who was working on his PhD, was instrumental in conceiving, planning and implementing the Year 7 Multimedia project. He was especially interested in how organisations like schools can effectively change their dominant culture. He argued that for significant change to occur, the whole culture needs to be involved. Hence, Ealing began with focus on Year 7, to be followed by incremental curriculum initiatives at each successive level, aimed at building on what had come earlier. By employing this strategy, Ealing's technology leaders anticipate the emergence of teachers and, by Year 12, students that are confident and adept in the use of the new technologies in all curriculum areas. According to the head of IT, when a project emerges from the curriculum framework the final product has greater meaning. An emphasis on technology alone results in a product that is more fragmented, not integrated and not connected to the education process. If by the end of Year 10 the students know how to use computers across the curriculum, they will be better equipped to face Years 11 and 12.

In the Year 7 Multimedia project the students used HyperCard, incorporating text, QuickTake photos, video clips, sound and animation. At the end of the year, students expressed a strong sense of achievement. The project's aim was for all the students to acquire skills and understanding and, even though the rate of learning varied from individual to individual, at its conclusion most of the students were competent with the technologies.

The experience cut two ways for participating English teachers. On one hand, it confirmed that multimedia may be an effective tool for learning. On the other hand, some teachers expressed concerns. One teacher said that all involved felt there was too much emphasis on graphics and drawings and not enough on the verbal text. Another felt multimedia's greatest advantage was in developing an understanding of narrative structures. Two believed that desktop publishing and word-processing had clear applications in English, but multimedia seemed less directly relevant. Another, who claimed that, despite school policy, technology was driving this curriculum initiative, also felt that technology was an add-on and not integral to a comprehensive English program. She argued that multimedia was different from the inclusion of film in the English curriculum. Film has a context, a theoretical base and an aesthetic, whereas multimedia has yet to develop these dimensions. She did acknowledge that the time was rapidly approaching when multimedia would assume an independent status and would need to be included in the curriculum. Central to the English teachers' ambivalence was the question: Is multimedia really English?

New Park Primary

New Park is located twenty kilometres from the central business district of a large state capital. More than 90 per cent of its 340 students are from language backgrounds other than English—Cambodian, Vietnamese, South American, Central American and Pacific Islander. Many families in the school community are refugees from war zones and are either unemployed or on low incomes. Very few students have computers in their homes. Students' access to technology is at school or in commercial venues such as video-game parlours.

Technology resourcing is a high priority in the budget, and had been since the mid-1980s under the leadership of the previous principal. Funded through the Disadvantaged Schools Program, New Park was able to acquire a computer laboratory, equipped with Apple IIes. Chris, a computer-savvy teacher, made it possible to continue to develop the lab and associated activities. He was put in charge of Computers in Education and maintains this role today.

The school's charter includes the aim to: 'enhance the Computer-Assisted Learning program which currently operates most effectively across all curriculum areas P–6 by extending and upgrading the already well-established computer laboratory and school-wide network system'. New Park's quite elaborate computer policy is designed to ensure that all students have access to computers in the lab at least once a week, a chance to use the mobile computers stored on trolleys at other times, and opportunities to engage with a range of software.

While the importance of technology is embedded in all curriculum policies, the practice at New Park does not reflect this. Except for two enthusiasts, the teachers at the school are not confident with technology and rarely use it. The principal observed that if he lost a few critically important people in one year, he would have a major crisis on his hands to maintain the program. Indeed, this was already foreshadowed at the time of the study. One of the enthusiasts, Stephanie, had successfully applied for another job, and the creative use of technology for language and literacy development that she initiated went into limbo. The principal expressed an urgency to 'skill up' all the teachers and give them a sense that they could 'do computers' as well. This, he said, was 'really hard work. The technology is developing so rapidly that if you are far behind, you feel as if you really can't keep up the pace'.

At the time of the study, Chris and Stephanie were the technology movers and shakers. Chris doubles as teacher-in-charge of computers and Year 5 teacher. His classroom is just down the hall from the computer lab. He is constantly called to solve problems as there is no other technical support within the school. For Chris, language is the central concern of New Park, and computers provide a catalyst for students to speak. As the students usually work in pairs, he argues that talk is promoted, except if they are word processing.

Stephanie prefers the term 'learning technologies' to 'computers', as it distinguishes what is happening in schools now from what previously occurred under 'computers in education'. She is also careful to use the word 'learning' rather than 'teaching', explaining that the computer does not teach students much. In her classes, the computer is presented as a 'vehicle for ideas,' like using a pencil, or paint or a camera'. Just like these other technologies, Stephanie believes that computers, particularly when supporting multimedia software, require the accumulation and manipulation of skills.

Each term, Stephanie undertakes a project with her Year 4 class using MicroWorlds, a multimedia programming package. She likes MicroWorlds, as it demonstrates that there are multiple ways of doing the same thing—of solving a problem. She tells us that multimedia draws on the students' visual principles, elicits talk, and encourages an 'embryonic understanding of music'. It also involves more traditional activities like writing, and its button-activated element entails new literacies. The fact that elements may be hidden means users must look for them.

New Park's students do not always have strength in English, although, as Stephanie puts it, they have 'all these good ideas inside them busting to get out'. Hence, she offers the students as many vehicles as possible to express ideas. Stephanie believes the students could learn considerably more using multimedia if they had access to it in subsequent years in the sorts of ways employed in her class. This, however, is unlikely under existing conditions. She regrets the ways CD-ROMs are used in other classes, where students seem mainly to be playing and filling in time. She regards such 'teaching' as unfocused—lacking real purpose and direction, and having little value for learners. According to Stephanie, entertainment is not what education should be about, and multimedia can and should be used in more educationally meaningful ways.

Stephanie exploits the potential of multimedia to enhance writing. While students would prefer to write direct to the screen, the fact that they access the computers only once a week means they must shape their stories ahead of time: planning in advance their titles, introductions to characters and settings, the story's body and three possible endings. The emphasis in story production is very much on text, with visuals serving mainly to enhance text. The students work in pairs, moving around the room at times to see what others are doing. Her class is characterised by a positive, open atmosphere and a learner-focused approach. There is a lot of peer teaching, with students typically on task. The following snapshot is indicative of computer-based lessons in Stephanie's Year 4 class:

The lesson gets underway with Stephanie reminding the class of what she wants them to focus on and achieve. Students listen carefully, but their eagerness to start on their stories is soon apparent. They are asked to work with a peer, check their texts for meaning, proof them, and then revise the procedures. The class is animated, abuzz, and students engage with each other's work showing enjoyment and interest. Stephanie operates as consultant, troubleshooter and energiser. She avoids making superficial comments, engaging with students' stories and working with them to ensure that the stories make sense. When the projects are completed Stephanie holds a 'show', projecting the work on the TV screen, observing that displaying stories in this public space stimulates the students to avoid mistakes and get their work looking good.

WHAT THESE PORTRAITS TELL US

While they represent just a tiny slice of technologised life in classrooms, the three portraits above nonetheless reflect features and patterns, issues and themes, that occur much more widely. In fact, they tell us quite a lot about where things currently are, in terms of new technologies in literacy education. We now pick out some of the features we find most illuminating in these portraits and comment on them briefly—as a way of laying a foundation for the remainder of the book. Some are widely recognised, others less so. Many of them overlap with and are related to other features.

Uneven development

Our examples reflect various kinds of 'unevenness'. For example, at Caldwell we saw a dramatic discrepancy between the computing infrastructure and aspirations within the school and the availability of crucial resources beyond the school. The school was equipped with internet capacity and the teachers were more than eager to make use of the internet in teaching and learning. But this was radically 'out of sync' with the telecommunications capacity of the 'bush telephone' network.

A second aspect of unevenness is readily apparent in terms of the distribution of resources and expertise within schools and between schools. At New Park, for instance, technical expertise was concentrated in just two of the staff. This resulted in one teacher becoming the 'fixit specialist' for the entire school—a well-known syndrome—and in a curriculum development project being put 'on ice' when the second expert got a new posting. At the level of resourcing, the discrepancy between schools like Ealing and the others reflects a well-known pattern.

A third kind of unevenness is evident in attitudes toward new technologies and their take-up by members of the same school staff. At New Park, for instance, only two teachers attempted to integrate technology into their curriculum planning and pedagogy in any systematic or ongoing way. The remainder were not very interested in what Chris and Stephanie were doing in their classes. While most were happy enough to take their students to the computer lab once a week, that was the extent of their involvement with new technologies.

Discontinuities and vulnerability

Our portraits provide examples of discontinuities and forms of vulnerability associated with uneven concentrations of human and non-human resources. At New Park, the students that happened to be placed in Stephanie's Year 4 class were privileged in their exposure to and experience of multimedia. They enjoyed a full and challenging year during which they acquired new skills and understandings of multiliteracy practices. This would probably be, however, a one-off experience. It was unlikely, when they progressed to Year 5 and then to Year 6, that they would have the opportunity to use multimedia again. This presents a particular challenge to schools. Developing effective portfolios of student learning outcomes involving literacy and new technologies depends vitally on continuity existing from point to point. This breaks down where, for instance, students do computing-rich work on a regular basis one year and miss out the next.

New Park highlights a further aspect of the vulnerability of technology initiatives—in this case, vulnerability to the departure of a key player. The story of Stephanie's Year 4 class, her significant achievements in the area of multimedia with a group of students in a school, with not inadequate resources but limited teacher expertise, and the virtual collapse of the multimedia program when she left for another job, exemplifies such vulnerability. The continued use of technology for literacy purposes at New Park was susceptible to disarray, even dismantlement, because it depended on two 'technology stars' who initiated and nurtured the activities. The rest of the teachers were less skilled, confident and motivated to explore the possible uses of the technologies in their own classes.

Caldwell provides an interesting example of another kind of vulnerability—this time in the form of 'susceptibility' to breakdowns, lack of coordination, or other contingencies within the 'system'. This occurred where the school, having established a site for computing activities and sorted out procedures that allowed students maximum access, suddenly lost its facility on the basis of student numbers. It then had to make an unsatisfactory short-term arrangement, before pursuing funding to get the school back to where it had been. What happened at Caldwell alerts us to a wider phenomenon, which has to do with various points in the education system operating in an 'articulation vacuum' with other points.

Doubts, suspicions, even fears

New technologies always generate a certain degree of suspicion and scepticism. They can prompt insecurity associated with exposure to the unfamiliar. This phenomenon is reflected in some interesting ways in our examples—again drawing attention to a wider syndrome that shows up under different headings below.

Two examples, rather different from each other, are especially interesting here. The first involves the sentiments expressed by some members of Caldwell's community in response to the teachers' enthusiasm to familarise their students with IT. Many of the parents were wary of the push for new technologies and their supposed educational benefits. Some openly expressed a fear of their children becoming smarter than they were. Elsewhere, doubts reflected the familiar argument that use of computers would lead to a decline in handwriting skills.

The second example illustrates the tendency for adults to see children as needing close surveillance when they are around new technologies. When the building was taken away, and students could no longer easily be observed from the staff room while at the computers during lunchtime and recess, the students were denied access because they could no longer be supervised. At the same time, it is important to note that the decision to restrict access was based also on safety and equity issues, not just on fear that damage to the technology might occur.

From the standpoint of the teachers, even those like the teachers at Caldwell, who were enthusiastic about new technologies, feelings of doubt were manifested in a deep sense of professional isolation. Ron and Carol both rued the absence of collegial support, although the appointment of a new regional consultant would alleviate at least some of their concern about access to technical expertise.

Culture clashes, competing values and resistance

The teachers in the portraits provided span a wide spectrum of attitudes and personal and professional positions, with respect to the significance and role of new technologies in classroom education. We found poles of enthusiasm and cynicism, plus plenty of examples of lukewarm to moderate interest.

Of particular significance are resistant responses that reflect strongly felt concerns, confusion, and even conflicts between competing sets of goals and values. These were most evident at Ealing among the English teachers. Despite the ready availability of training opportunities and ample technological support in the classrooms, the English teachers were still resistant to using the technologies. Some argued that the Year 7 Multimedia project compromised what is central to English as a key learning area—the printed text. These teachers regarded the visual as secondary to subject English and thought the students wasted valuable time incorporating visual information into their multimedia texts.

There was a further dimension to tensions surrounding the place of new technologies in literacy education evident at Ealing. This had to do with the amount of time teachers should have to spend on teaching students how to use the technologies competently. Although the English teachers recognised that acquiring technological literacies was part of being multiliterate, they resented the time it took away from other parts of the syllabus. But, at the same time as they talked of pressure imposed on them to acquire and teach students new skills, the teachers said they could not ignore the social and cultural demands to familiarise students with the new technologies. Like the teachers at Caldwell, they believed that it was the school's responsibility to prepare students for the world beyond school, and that technology was central to that world. The Computer Awareness teacher for Years 7 and 8 at Ealing talked specifically of preparing students 'to work in non-linear environments': to learn how to skim; to work in a layered way; to evaluate critically; to read the visual; to select valuable resources from the web. These skills represented the new literacies—the technoliteracies—that students needed to cope in a changing literacy world.

Strategies for development and change

The three portraits reflect very different approaches to tackling the challenge to classroom learning posed by the technologising of social life. In the 'micro-school' environment of Caldwell, there is no formal policy governing technology and literacy. The principal assumes responsibility for generally keeping up with developments in the area and for making budget decisions related to resourcing. Beyond that, he takes advice from a regional consultant. With only one other teacher at the school sharing the principal's interest, general competence and standpoint on technology and learning, Caldwell seems content to maintain a 'steady as we go' approach, tackling issues as they arise.

New Park occupies an intermediate position. It has quite an elaborate computer policy, a clear aim expressed in its charter to enhance the school's computer-assisted learning program, and a well-established commitment to prioritising technology resourcing in the budget. It does not, however, have a strategy in place for developing an across-the-school culture of integrating new technologies into learning. The principal would have liked to implement a whole-school approach to literacy and technology, and the school's charter enshrined such an approach as a possibility. But only two teachers in a staff of 23 were to any extent interested in exploring the potential of new technologies for teaching and learning.

At the other pole we find Ealing, which has a sophisticated and highly 'contemporary' corporate-style strategy for building a culture. Beginning in the late 1970s, Ealing adopted a whole-school approach that has been carefully conceived, planned and implemented. The school found solutions to many of the problems that continue to plague other settings: strong leadership, assiduous planning, mutually beneficial connections with the corporate sector, consultation rather than imposition of IT policy, clear IT curriculum objectives, and in-house professional development. The program was not person-dependent. The use of the new technologies was so deeply imbricated across the curriculum that it would probably continue, no matter who left.

Planning was central to Ealing's approach to the integration of literacy, technology and learning. There was a lot of preparation and groundwork done before the enhanced internet facilities were set up: there were meetings, as well as discussions and exploration of the potential of the internet in particular subject areas.

Interestingly, the principal of Ealing had not intervened directly in decisions about technology. He had particular trust in the head of Computing, the head of IT and the curriculum coordinator, who worked as a team to implement change. By identifying a key person in each subject area and working with these individuals in the development of skills with the new technologies, the three leaders initiated change and development in particular curriculum areas. When it came to 'encouraging' the English teachers to become more actively involved, the curriculum coordinator's solution was to 'inspire' them and to supply the 'adrenalin'. She was not concerned that the English teachers continued to privilege the printed text, so long as they understood that other forms of text were possible, important and needed to be included in the English curriculum. She also argued that the English teachers needed to extend their role of teaching critical skills to navigate the new literacy spaces presented by the internet. At the same time, there was a recognition at Ealing that all teachers across the curriculum were responsible for teaching students critical literacy skills—to question texts and authors, and to assess the credibility of sources.

It is salutary to observe how this kind of strategising worked and its effect. When we returned to Ealing, six months after collecting the data to discuss with the key informants their responses to the first draft of our write-up, we were told of several interesting developments. First, as a result of the Year 7 Multimedia project, the head of English had become so engaged with the possibilities of hypertext in the teaching of literature that she had asked her Year 11 students to design webs in response to the text under study. She emphasised that the literary text was still at the centre of her work with the students; however, she was now encouraging the students to use a range of media to explore the meanings of the text and its connections with other texts.

Second, the English teachers were planning to develop web pages with their classes that would serve as professional development for themselves and represent a curriculum initiative. The head of English had been transformed, from a person who was perhaps appropriately sceptical and cautious about the place of technology in English to an enthusiast, using the internet for her own purposes and not just for school-related projects.

Business as usual

Although the literacy activities involving new technologies in these three sites varied to some extent, they were predictable and characteristically 'school-like'. In the snapshots described from the classroom observations, we found students on computers writing stories, illustrating Christmas cards, using Treasure Maths, producing multimedia versions of a myth, and creating still more narratives. In many cases, as occurs in many schools and classrooms, this work involves using computers to transcribe work already drafted with pens and pencils.

To a large extent, the substance of learning and teaching remains more or less the same as it was in the 'pre-computer era', only now 'technologised' under a new technology regime, machines having displaced pens. This has been referred to as the 'old wine in new bottles' syndrome. Our portraits support Seymour Papert's (1993) wry observation that time travellers from the 19th century could step into a contemporary classroom and know at a glance where they were. They also lend weight to Steven Hodas' arguments about the capacity of classrooms to shape successive technologies to familiar classroom forms (Hodas 1996).

We believe that in part this reflects pressure on resources. Stephanie, for example, made it clear that at New Park she would prefer to have the students compose directly to the screen, but limited access to computers precluded this. By the same token, even if the students were to compose directly to the screen, the activity would amount to little more than the electronic production of traditional school fare. We believe, rather, that some of what we saw in the way of computer-mediated activity has to do with the fact that teachers still have limited experience of 'real-life' developments and applications of new technologies occurring beyond the school gates. To this extent, we should not expect to see strikingly innovative applications.

There are, of course, further points to consider. Many teachers are quite unfamiliar with new technologies, hence they spend a lot of time and energy learning, as it were, how to press the buttons. Not surprisingly, they often do this in the context of classroom routines with which they are familiar. Beyond this, there is the obvious fact that teachers are not the only players who shape what goes on in classrooms. Unless and until curriculum and syllabus guidelines and educational goals and directions emanating from outside the schools offer wider visions of what school learning is about, we should perhaps not expect any more than our portraits afford. Indeed, so far as the current National Literacy Plan (DEETYA 1998) goes, we might, if anything, expect even less.

2 Understanding the changing world of literacy, technology and learning

In chapter 1 we present some typical portraits or sketches of life in the changing world of literacy education. Within this dynamic context, teachers are being challenged to think and act in new ways about literacy, technology and learning. Very often, teachers find themselves having to respond to the new demands without the necessary resources to assist them. With limitations on time, space to think, local expertise, models of good practice, sound information, technical support or clear policy directions, an already tough job becomes even tougher.

For many teachers, including several in our study, the task of trying to integrate new technologies into literacy education in meaningful and effective ways is something they tackle 'on the run'—making it up as they go along, grabbing ideas where they can find them. Typically the teachers we observed did this in the midst of competing demands, often in settings complicated by the already familiar features of the times in which we live. These features include culturally diverse student populations, multiple linguistic differences within the classroom, intensified demands for reporting and assessment, a turbulent policy environment, and changing teacher roles and responsibilities associated with self-managing schools.

This chapter offers some ideas we believe will be useful to literacy teachers in this challenging and changing context. Not surprisingly, time and again in our study we found teachers thinking about literacy in established and familiar ways, trying to incorporate new technologies into conventional frameworks. Unfortunately, this is not tenable. Literacies and literacy demands are changing in our midst. We need to understand the forces of change influencing the world of literacy education if we are to respond effectively—which, we would add, does not mean simply following trends manifest in the world beyond schooling. Similarly, we found teachers thinking about technologies mainly in terms of specific tools and techniques, and about learning in terms of familiar classroom approaches and purposes. In this chapter we present different conceptions of literacy, technology and learning from those we encountered in the schools and classrooms observed in our study. We also suggest how these three concepts can be seen as related in ways that helpfully inform teaching and learning.

But before we present our ideas about literacy, technology and learning it is important to explain why this is no simple task. In the first place, while the three terms are common in everyday thinking and usage, they are understood in different ways by different people. Second, although they are often thought and spoken about separately from one another, we know that all such concepts are never self-contained: rather, they are defined in relation to each other, as well as to other concepts. Third, they are highly contested. They are not notions like 'triangle' or 'stanza', which command a fair degree of agreement about meaning. Even though 'triangle' and 'stanza' presuppose some kind of cultural and discursive view, this is nothing compared to what is at stake with notions such as 'literacy', 'technology' and 'learning'. These three terms are intensely value-laden—contaminated by what people variously aspire to and hold important. It follows that our account of literacy, technology and learning is unlikely to be universally accepted. Indeed, in the contrasting classrooms we visited and in the policy documents and wider literature we consulted, we constantly found them to be contested. Different people understood all three in different and sometimes radically divergent ways.

LITERACY

During recent years, the rapid rate of growth of computer use in literacy education has been accompanied by two widely held beliefs: one is that literacy is now having technology added to it—that is, literacy is becoming technological; the other is that new communication and information technologies provide new ways of 'doing' literacy. Yet, despite the emergence of new ways of thinking about literacy, literacy education remains much the same enterprise as it has always been. Literacy education continues to involve students learning and using 'old skills', but 'applying them in new ways' via new technologies and new media. These old skills using new technologies include: being able to decode and encode fluently; using literacy abilities and understandings involved in researching and reporting information; reading and deciding what is relevant; note-taking, scanning, and collecting information in a selective way.

The current historical moment, however, challenges us to think about literacy and technology differently. First, if we think of literacy as 'language made visible'—as written or encoded language—it is obvious that literacy always involves some kind of technology or other. What literacy is in a particular time and place is necessarily related to the technologies available locally. Literacy and technology are always integrally related. Written language is always already technologised, in the sense that it comes into being only in and through available technologies of information and communication—such as marks on natural surfaces, the alphabet and other symbol systems, stylus and pencil, the printing press and, today, the 'digital-electronic apparatus' (Bigum & Green 1992; Snyder 1996). Yet, as Chip Bruce observes, typically we 'don't notice the technologies of literacy because we treat our literacy technologies as natural and inevitable' (Bruce 1998: 47). Just as we assume that writing is something that is done with pen and paper, chalk and blackboard, typewriter or word processor, so people in earlier times would scarcely have imagined writing by means other than sharpened stone, burned stick, stylus or quill (see Durrant & Green 1998). And how people wrote, how much they wrote, what they wrote, why they wrote, who could read what they wrote, and when they wrote, varied in association with the literacy technology they were using.

Second, we must recognise that literacy is not fixed but is ever-evolving; literacy is always changing. When we take a historical perspective, we see immediately that as technologies change it is not at all a matter of people continuing to use the same old skills, merely of applying them in different ways. As Figure 1 indicates, in the case of literacy as much as with any other social practice successive advances in technology have extended the boundaries of what previously was possible. And each technological advance has

Figure 1   Literacy transformations

→ Primitive symbol systems
    → Complex oral language
        → Early writing
            → Manuscript literacy
                → Print literacy
                    → Video literacy
                        → Digital/multimedia/hypertext literacy
                            → Virtual reality

Source: Bruce 1998: 47

seen a corresponding change in how we practise literacy and understand its social role.

Today, as much as in any other historical period, the development of new technologies has implications for changing forms and practices of literacy. Rather than thinking in terms of old skills being expressed through new media, and of trying to 'squeeze' new technologies into familiar ways of doing the 'literacy education business', we need to attend to the reality of new and emerging literacies and new modes of human practice and ways of experiencing the world (Green & Bigum 1993; Snyder 1996, 1997). Whether we are conscious of it and take it into account or not, 'the creation of new technologies continues to change society's concept of literacy, just as it has always done' (Durrant & Green 1998: 3).

As far as schooling is concerned, print is just one medium of literate practice within an entire range of available media. And the centre of gravity is shifting. We are in the midst of 'a broad-based shift from Print to Digital-Electronics as the organising context for literate-textual practice and for learning and teaching' (Durrant & Green 1998: 1). While this does not mean the end of print—the death of the book—it certainly means that teachers need to adopt a more flexible and expansive view of literacy than they have needed in their everyday lives and work to date. We are fast moving beyond the bounds of print-based literacy. We should, as teachers, both recognise this profound cultural shift and be positioning ourselves to take advantage of what is and can become possible with each technological advance. However, as we have suggested already, this does not mean 'enthusiastically and, perhaps, ingenuously veer[ing] into every newly enticing detour on the information superhighway'—rather, that 'nothing should be necessarily eliminated from our lists of items of potential usefulness just because it does not fit our current notions of literacy' (Durrant & Green 1998: 3).

In current times, literacy teachers need an approach that asks, openly and seriously: Just how do we go about shifting our strategies for teaching more or less print-bound literacy to helping our students meet the fresh demands and challenges of literacies that spring from living in such technologised and seamless times (Durrant & Green 1998)? This is not to suggest that the printed word, in the printed book, is no longer important for literacy education, but that its importance is 'being *transformed* in relation to new technologies, new cultures, and new forms of life' (Durrant & Green 1998: 5). Further, the challenges facing literacy teachers require taking account not only of the changing circumstances and conditions of literacy, learning and schooling, but also of those enduring educational and social issues to do with fair and reasonable forms of access and equity, and opportunities for designing and shaping the future (Kress 1995). We look at what all this means below, in practice as well as in our thinking and professional development; meanwhile, we point it out at this stage as a necessary perspective for literacy teachers to adopt.

A sociocultural perspective

While current technological changes and related changes in social practices beyond the school are now forcing us to challenge some of our conventional assumptions about literacy, another challenge to long-held beliefs about literacy has been developing within literacy theory since the 1960s and 70s. This is what has become known as a 'sociocultural approach' to literacy.

Traditionally, literacy has been thought of 'as a largely *psychological* ability—something true about our heads' (Gee, Hull & Lankshear 1996: 1). That is, to become literate is to have something done to our brains, so that we achieve a special kind of cognitive 'faculty' or inner capacity. This view reflects the domination of psychology in educational theory and research throughout this century. Being literate has been seen as a matter of cracking the alphabetic code, word-formation skills, phonics, grammar, and comprehension skills. According to this view, encoding and decoding skills serve as building blocks for doing other things and for accessing meanings. For instance, once people are literate, they can get on with learning through the medium of texts—by studying subjects in a curriculum, or by other print-mediated means. When people are literate, they can use 'it' (the skill repertoire, the ability) as a 'tool' to pursue all sorts of 'goods' (employment, knowledge, recreational pleasure, personal development, economic growth, innovation). But to 'get literate' in the first place is seen from this perspective as a matter of inserting the necessary skills into people's heads. There are debates about how best to achieve this (for example, phonics, letter recognition, 'letter chunking'), but those debating the most effective way all share the idea of literacy as basically a 'head thing', a psychological ability.

By contrast, understanding literacy as sociocultural practice means that reading and writing can be understood and acquired only within the context of the social, cultural, political, economic and historical practices to which they are integral. This idea was captured by Brian Street's (1984) distinction between the 'autnonomous' and 'ideological' models of literacy. Incidentally, the 'sociocultural practice' view of human activity applies equally well to literacy, technology and learning. From the sociocultural standpoint, literacy is best understood as 'shorthand for the social practices of reading and writing' (Street 1984: 1). As such, literacy is really 'literacies', as print-based activities take many different forms—some of which are very unlike others in terms of purposes and the kinds of texts involved. According to a sociocultural approach, these differences must be seen as residing in the literacies themselves, rather than outside or independently of them, as we never learn, teach or employ literacy 'skills' in context-free ways, but always within some context of practice. Different social practices—different contexts of practice—'embed' different forms of literacy.

The relationship between human practice and producing and sharing meanings underlies the sociocultural view. Human practices are meaningful ways of doing things, of getting things done (Franklin 1990). For example, social practices of cooking–feeding–eating are not mere 'biologically necessary acts'. They are saturated with cultural meanings, and different groups practise 'cooking–feeding–eating' in different ways. The practice (not one practice, in fact, but many practices) means different things to different groups. And these different meanings do not exist just in the head, and are not produced just in the head. There is a head component, of course, but the 'meaning-making' is based largely in the material practices that take place in the social-cultural settings of the groups involved.

According to the sociocultural view, the same is true for literacy as for practices like cooking–feeding–eating. Reading or writing is always reading or writing something in particular with under-standing. Different kinds of text require 'somewhat different backgrounds and somewhat different skills' if they are to be read meaningfully. Moreover, particular texts can be read in different ways, depending on the different practices in which these texts occur. For instance, Christians from different denominations may, and often do, read 'the same texts' from the Bible in radically different ways. Similarly, the meanings of the word 'joint' are very different for the joiner or carpenter, the butcher, and the hippie or Rastafarian, as are the wider meanings of the word 'joint' within the three Discourses in question.

A key idea here, and one to which we return in later chapters, is captured in James Gee's (1996) distinction between 'Discourses' and 'discourses'. With an upper-case 'D', Discourses are human practices which bring together and combine such things as beliefs, actions, values, world views, goals and purposes, standards, ways of dressing and gesturing, ways of behaving appropriately, as well as ways of speaking, reading and writing. We all 'belong' to numerous Discourses, and different people belong to different sets of Discourses—which is why people are different. It is through recruitment into and participation in Discourses that we acquire and develop our identities. To be in the teaching Discourse means to do the things teachers do in the ways that they do them. Of course, there are variations here—teaching assumes somewhat different forms and somewhat different details from place to place; however, we can generally agree when we come across instances of teaching Discourses.

With a lower-case 'd', discourses refer to the language 'bits' within Discourses (Gee 1996). Every Discourse is mediated by ways of using language—written, spoken, gestural—that make sense within that Discourse. Gee defines 'discourses' as 'connected stretches of language that make sense' (1996: 127). The point about 'discourses', however, is that they vary from Discourse to Discourse. And part of what is involved in learning to operate effectively within a Discourse is to become fluent and appropriate in its discourse.

This always involves more than just coming to grips with 'technical' or 'skills' aspects like encoding and decoding. Learning how to handle the reading and writing components of a Discourse requires being immersed in social practices where participants 'not only *read* texts of this type in this way but also *talk* about such texts in certain ways, *hold certain attitudes and values* about them, and *socially interact* over them in certain ways' (Gee, Hull & Lankshear 1996: 3). For instance, people participating in the university Discourse of English Literature are recruited into doing very different things in very different ways with *Great Expectations* than, say, a caregiver and child might when reading Dickens at bedtime. Indeed, the versions of the text might even be different (for example, a talking book version, a Reader's Digest condensed version, or the Everyman edition).

People who have different histories of 'immersion' in Discourses acquire different forms of reading and writing as practice. Every meaningful text we read and write is an integral—embedded—element of some Discourse or other. In Gee's words, every meaningful text we read is an integral or embedded element of some 'lived, talked, enacted, value-and-belief-laden practice', which is engaged in under specific conditions, at specific times and in specific places (1996: 3). Therefore, it is impossible to abstract or decontextualise 'literacy bits' from the larger practices in which they are embedded and for them still to mean what they mean in real life. Seen in this way, it suddenly seems very odd to think that we could teach people to read and write by 'attending to their heads'—by teaching literacy 'skills' outside contexts of 'authentic' social practices. Yet this is precisely what is presumed by the 'one size fits all' view of literacy education that prevails in school education.

By contrast, a sociocultural perspective suggests that literacy should be seen as having three interlocking dimensions or aspects of learning and practice—the operational, the cultural, and the critical. These three dimensions bring together language, meaning and context (Green 1988). The key point to recognise here is that none of these dimensions of discourse and practice has any necessary priority over the others. In an integrated view of literate practice and literacy pedagogy, all dimensions need to be taken into account simultaneously. This means that it is counterproductive to begin with issues of skills outside of an 'authentic' context of social practice. Importantly, this principle holds for all learning—in both formal and informal settings, for people of all ages, across all curriculum areas.

The 'operational' dimension of literacy includes but also goes beyond competence with the tools, procedures and techniques involved in being able to handle the written language system proficiently, for it is through the medium of language that the literacy event happens. The operational dimension is a matter of individuals being able to read and write in a range of contexts, in an appropriate and adequate manner. This is to focus on the language aspect of literacy (Green 1988, 1997a, 1997b).

The 'cultural' dimension involves competence with the meaning system of a practice: knowing what it means to be 'in' this practice/

Discourse, and how to make and grasp meanings appropriately within the practice. It is never simply a case of being literate, but of being literate with regard to something, some aspect of knowledge or experience. The cultural aspect of literacy is a matter of understanding texts in relation to contexts—to appreciate their meaning; the meaning they need to carry to be appropriate; and what it is about given contexts of practice that makes for appropriateness or inappropriateness of particular ways of reading and writing. It recognises that literacy is always more than just being able to operate language and technology systems: such operational capacities are always in the service of 'authentic' forms of meaning and practice. Take, for example, the case of a worker producing a spreadsheet within a workplace setting or routine. This is not a simple matter of 'going into some software program' and 'filling in the data'. Spreadsheets must be compiled—which means knowing their purpose and constructing their axes and categories accordingly. To know the purpose of a particular spreadsheet requires understanding relevant elements of the culture of the immediate work context; to know why one is doing what one is doing now, how to do it, and why what one is doing is appropriate (Gee, Hull & Lankshear 1996). To focus on the cultural dimension of literacy is to focus on matters of practice and meaning (Durrant & Green 1998).

The 'critical' dimension involves awareness that all social practices, and hence all literacies, are socially constructed and 'selective': they include some representations and classifications—values, purposes, rules, standards, perspectives—and exclude others. To participate effectively and productively in any literate practice, people must be socialised into it. But if individuals are socialised into a literacy without realising that it is socially constructed and selective, and also that it can be acted on and transformed, they cannot play an active role in changing it. The critical dimension of literacy is the basis for ensuring that individuals are not merely able to participate in an existing literacy and make meanings within it, but also that, in various ways, they are able to transform and actively produce it (Green 1988; Gee, Hull & Lankshear 1996).

Rather than focusing on 'how-to' knowledge, as it usually is understood—that is, as technical competence or so-called 'functional literacy'—the three-dimensional model of literacy complements and supplements technical competence by contextualising it, with due regard for matters of culture, history and power. The 3D model is a holistic, culturally critical view of literacy–technology learning that takes explicit account of contexts, contextuality and contextualisation

(Lemke 1995). It compels us to attend to context, and to its significance in terms of meaning and power.

TECHNOLOGY

It is still common for teachers to think of technology in terms of tools and implements. This is true in the case of all the new electronic communication and information technologies; it is especially true in the case of computers. However, as we have seen in our discussion of literacy, a narrow view of technology can impede our understanding of key ideas such as the inherently technological and changing nature of literacies. It follows that concentrating only on the tools or implements aspect of technology can blind us to its important social and cultural dimensions, and, in particular, to recognising technology as social practice. Understanding technology, and technologies, in terms of social practice is very helpful in the context of education. This is not to say that it is wrong to identify technology with tools and applications and gadgets—only that it can be limiting.

Technology practice

Arnold Pacey's (1983) concept of 'technology practice' is useful in helping us to recognise that technology is a form of social practice and not, as is so often assumed, culturally neutral (see Idhe 1990). When we look at a machine such as a computer, the opposite may seem to be true. However, once we consider the web of human activities surrounding the computer's use, we soon realise that technology is part of life itself and not something that can be kept in a separate compartment.

According to Pacey, the problem is that 'technology' has become a catchword with a confusion of different meanings—not unlike the situation with 'literacy', described in the previous section. But correct usage is not beyond recovery if we look to the field of medicine. The distinction is often made 'by talking about "medical practice" when a general term is required, and employing the phrase "medical science" for the more strictly technical aspects of the subject' (Pacey 1983: 3). The term 'medical practice' refers to the whole activity of medicine, 'including its basis in technical knowledge, its organisation, and its cultural aspects' (1983: 3). The cultural aspects include the sense of vocation, the values, and the satisfactions shared by doctors and the ethical code of their profession.

Even when 'medical practice' in different countries, regions and localities draws on much the same base of 'medical science'—knowledge, theory, techniques, instruments—Pacey observes that medical practice can still take on very different forms. The explanation is that there is much more to medical practice than the scientific-technical base alone: medical practice goes on within organisational set-ups and within cultural frameworks. For instance, the organisational set-ups may range from private medicine to public medicine, from free market provision to welfare state provision, from centralised control and planning to local control and planning, from planned provision to ad-hoc provision. Thus defined, 'practice' becomes a broad and inclusive concept. Building on this model, Pacey sees 'technology practice' as 'the application of scientific and other knowledge to practical tasks by ordered systems that involve people and organisations, living things and machines' (1983: 6). That is, technology practice has technical, organisational and cultural dimensions. To think of technology in terms of tools, implements, techniques and knowhow alone is to limit our conception of technology to one of its three component dimensions—what Pacey calls 'the technical'. As Pacey explains diagramatically, technology practice refers to everything that goes on within a triangle, the three points of which are defined by the organisational, cultural, and technical dimensions of human technological activity (see Figure 2).

Pacey's model of technology practice has some interesting implications when we apply it to the nexus between classrooms and new communication and information technologies. Consider, for example, email and the internet. In *Where Wizards Stay up Late*, Katie Hafner and Matthew Lyon (1996) provide an account of the development of electronic mail and the birth of the internet. They take us into the workplaces, lives and beliefs of people employed by the Pentagon at the height of the Cold War to develop a new kind of communications system for the US Defense Department. We are given an inside look at the technical, organisational and cultural dimensions of the project that yielded, as products, tools and techniques, prototype electronic mail applications and an internet to support them—in effect, Pacey's technology practice in action. We can see email and the internet as outcomes of scientific and other forms of knowledge (management knowledge, financial knowledge, mathematical knowledge, systems theory), as the result of a practical task (defence communications), by an ordered system

Figure 2   Diagrammatic definitions of 'technology' and 'technology practice'

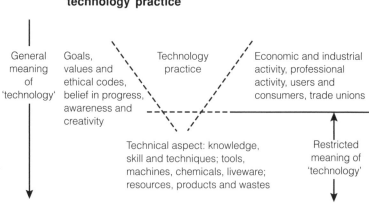

General meaning of 'technology'	Goals, values and ethical codes, belief in progress, awareness and creativity	Technology practice	Economic and industrial activity, professional activity, users and consumers, trade unions

Technical aspect: knowledge, skill and techniques; tools, machines, chemicals, liveware; resources, products and wastes

Restricted meaning of 'technology'

Source: Pacey 1983: 6

(created and managed by the Advanced Research Projects Agency within the US Defense Department) involving people (programmers, designers), organisations (contracted and subcontracted companies, phone companies), and machines.

After reading Hafner and Lyon's account, it is impossible to view email and the internet merely as 'tools' or 'applications'. In their prototypical forms, they were saturated with human ideas and ideals, with tensions and anxieties, hopes and aspirations, values and purposes, targets and deadlines, dreams and nightmares—none of which had anything to do with classrooms, literacy education, school-based learning, curriculum planning and timetabling. Email and the internet were designed for altogether different purposes. And the same kind of story can be told for the computer itself, as well as for HyperCard, Word, PowerPoint and HTML. What we can begin to see is that in taking these applications into classrooms, we are necessarily 'remaking them' into a different kind of 'tool', to serve different purposes, within different systems, inhabited by different people, bearing different cultural goals and values, informed by different elements of knowledge, skills and techniques.

We might well ask:

- Why are we doing this?
- When is it a good idea to do this?
- What can we sensibly do with this facility?
- How does it affect our practice?

- In what ways does it influence what our students and we become as people, as literate persons, as knowers?
- How do we evaluate it?
- How do we rank it in relation to our educational priorities?
- Whose interests are served by the efforts of people like us to integrate these new technological applications into our literacy programs?
- What kind of world are we contributing to building by taking up this technology?
- What other things will we need to do to help prepare today's learners to live in this world?

Many teachers and administrators in diverse schools and school systems are well aware of the need to ask such questions—even if their awareness does not necessarily spring from interrogating the idea of technology as we have done here. In the widest sense, new communication and information technologies refer to the revolutionary 'coming together of publishing, broadcasting, computing and telecommunications in the form of digital global media networks' (Green & Bigum 1993; Green 1997b). These networks are connected with new institutional practices in business, education, finance, administration and management, and manufacture, and with new ways of experiencing the world, and new places from which to experience it. As the changes are occurring rapidly and on an ever-increasing scale, we have to reimagine and reinvent ourselves and our institutions. These new ways of thinking involve, among other things, coming to terms with reimagined and reinvented forms of literacy, subject matter and learning.

Reconceiving our schools and our teaching practices, however, must not be done 'blind', without careful reflection. Just as we must assume a socially critical stance toward literacy and technology in the broadest sense, we need to adopt a socially critical stance toward communication and information technologies, taking careful account of their educational applications and implications. As we have argued, a critical stance means understanding the place of new technologies within contemporary history and culture and in relation to ourselves and everyday social practice. It means adopting a kind of orientation and attitude towards new technologies and developing understandings and skills, which involves more than simply 'learning how to drive them'. Teachers need 'to become appropriately informed and skilled with regard to new technologies, which . . . means becoming critical consumers or users'. In essence, it means assuming the role of critically informed 'insiders' (Bigum & Green 1995: 13).

The Resource-Context model

In considering what becoming a critical user involves, a Resource-Context model of new technologies, advanced by Chris Bigum and Bill Green (1995), provides a helpful adjunct to Pacey's (1983) notion of technology practice. This model can be approached via Sproull and Kiesler's two-level perspective on technologies, based on their idea of 'first and second level effects' (Sproull & Kiesler 1991).

'First-level' effects refer to planned or anticipated benefits when new technologies are implemented—for example, in terms of productivity or efficiency gains. First-level effects can be gauged using such conventions as cost-displacement analysis or value-added analysis. When we think of new technologies as 'Resource' within educational settings, we have in mind using them to produce beneficial effects. In the case of literacy education, often claimed first-level effects include increased student motivation and pride in work and enhanced learning outcomes for disabled learners.

'Second-level' effects relate to 'Context'. They include changes in environments of social practice (for example, classrooms, offices) and in practices themselves (for example, teaching, learning, administering, accounting) which result from participants actually using the technologies. When new technologies are introduced into sites of practice, they change the social circumstances within which they are used. The result is often a change in the ways in which people talk and think about them. One important consequence of these changes is that social practitioners use new technologies in ways that are often different, unanticipated and unpredictable.

The relationship between Resource and Context goes in two directions and is dynamic: it has a 'both-ways' logic. If we represented the Resource-Context model as a diagram, it would resemble a feedback loop. Using new technologies (as Resource) produces changes within settings (Context). These changes act back on subsequent uses (Resource), which in turn act back on the settings (Context), including on our expectations, aspirations, beliefs and purposes (Bigum & Green 1995; Lankshear et al. 1997; Sproull & Kiesler 1991).

The Resource-Context model is pertinent to developing the socially critical, informed stance literacy teachers need to become 'insiders' when using communication and information technologies in teaching and learning. In most settings, including educational settings, new technologies are 'sold' to us initially, on the basis of their alleged first-level effects: the benefits, we are told, that will result from using them as Resource. However, because of the inescapable 'feedback loop' relationship between new technologies, as both Resource and Context, the claims used to support the adoption, purchase and implementation of a given technology are difficult to substantiate before they have actually been used. The bottom line is that too often decisions about the adoption and use of communication and information technologies in schools are based not on what we know about their benefits and limitations, but on unsubstantiated claims about their capacity to enhance teaching and learning.

Bringing Resource and Context together in this reciprocal and dynamic way helps us to achieve more comprehensive and informed views of what integrating new technologies into literacy work actually means in terms of social practice. In assessing what it means, we must consider risk factors and potential 'negatives', as well as promises and possibilities. As Bigum and Green (1995) observe, the advantages associated with communication and information technologies must always be taken into account and assessed in tandem with their disadvantages. The difficulty for literacy teachers is that not all the outcomes can be known in advance. Indeed, each new technology has to be socially reinvented at each new site of use.

In these terms, the history of the new information and communication technologies in Australian schools has been characterised by large quantities of faith, with returns that are at best difficult to identify. Confounding identification in a school setting is the presence of another powerful technology, that of the school itself (Green & Bigum 1998). To a large extent—as is evident in the portraits of classrooms provided in chapters 1 and 4—computers get 'schooled'. They get made into things that support and sustain the technology that is the school. As Stephen Hodas (1996: 217) argues:

> The norms and procedures of entrenched bureaucratic organizations are strong and self-reinforcing. They attract people of like minds and repel or expel those who don't share them. Schools are technologies, machines with a purpose. They embed the norms and processes in their outputs, which in the case of schools helps them to further strengthen their cultural position and resist marginalization.

The relationship between literacy and text

As we discuss in the next section on 'learning', some of the strong and entrenched norms and procedures of school approaches to teaching and learning need to be seriously rethought in relation to literacy and technology if the integration of new technologies into literacy education is to be as effective as is possible and desirable.

We will also need to rethink our familiar, established ways of associating literacy and text (Green & Bigum 1996; Peters & Lankshear 1996). The link between these ideas is so close that literacy is often practically defined in terms of text: for example, in text-context models of literacy, in conceptions of literacy that focus on text-reader roles, and in theories that explore text-mediated meaning-making. The arrival of new communication and information technologies, however, challenges conventional ways of thinking about literacy in terms of text, as well as challenging our very idea of text(s) per se. Many writers, including literacy theorists such as Gunther Kress (1995) and Jay Lemke (1995), have identified the need to question and extend our existing ideas of text and literacy. Is 'the text metaphor' (Morgan 1996) adequate or even appropriate for understanding multimedia practices, information flows, or mean-ing-making practices in general within a dramatically mutating 'semiotic landscape' (Kress 1995: 25)? Does text encompass image? Sound? Multimodality? Non-linearity (Snyder 1996)?

Our existing idea of text is based in the technology of print, the era of the printing press. As such, we think of texts as 'bounded'. In the print era, all instances of encoded information and commu-nication were bounded. That was their only form—a physical text of some kind. In the print era, texts have edges, borders, margins: the very condition of print (Tuman 1992). But with the shift from print technology to computing, and the emergence of database technology, hypertext and hypermedia, we can now ask: Where is the text? Indeed, more radically and unusually, we can ask: When is the text? also: What is the text? Which is text and which is context? If we take the example of the database: Is the text the database as a whole? If so, what about open-ended, relational, networked databases? Is the text an individual report? Is it the program? How do we distinguish the text from the content? The problem is that 'inside' the database—wherever and whatever it is—there are no distinctions: everything is digitalised and virtualised.

This quantum difference from the mechanics of print calls for radically new ways of thinking about all sorts of things in the world, not just texts. Electronic apparatuses are profoundly different from mechanical apparatuses, and with these differences come different ways of understanding and experiencing 'reality'. Reality itself changes. Something happens to how we perceive and experience time, for instance, when the 'timepiece norm' changes from hourglass to mechanical watch or clock, to some form of digital LCD unit. As for time, so for language, communication and literacy. But in literacy education, these matters remain embryonic, despite the fact that a generation of young people have already been born into a world where digital-electronic 'ontology' and 'subjectivity' have become the norm, at least in countries like Australia, Britain, Canada, New Zealand and the USA. The titles of three books, which explore new forms of reality and identity in electronic times, capture the essence of some of these shifts: Nicholas Negroponte's (1996) *Being Digital*, Sherry Turkle's (1995) *Life on the Screen* and Ilana Snyder's *Page to Screen* (Snyder 1997).

Within literacy education, the impact of these changes goes far beyond questions about the nature of text and the relationship between literacy and text. It goes deep into the realm of values, norms, priorities, goals and purposes, and identities. For example, it was not simply that literacy and literacy education had become tied to the notion of text within formal education during the print era. In many ways, the text paradigm was the literary text, and essayist writing dominated school literacy. However, what we now see emerging in the context of the burgeoning presence of electronic information technologies is the separation of text and information and a need for us to view literacy as involving, even requiring, the integration of text and information. This notion challenges traditional ways of thinking about literacy that have conceived of texts largely as encompassing, or subsuming, information. According to this view, information has been seen as subordinate; 'information' is secondary to 'understanding', or to usage. The trouble is that 'information has become a privileged term in our culture' and 'the current culture gives a certain fetishistic importance to "information"' (Poster 1990: 6–7).

The new privileged status of information confronts head-on the liberal-humanist tradition of literacy theory and pedagogy. For instance, an exemplary exponent of this influential tradition, Frank Smith, proposed his preferred view of literacy as 'creating worlds' in opposition to what he saw as the increasingly dominant view— that of 'shunting information'. 'The creation of worlds', argued Smith (1985: 197), 'is a more productive and appropriate metaphor for

Figure 3   Literate practice

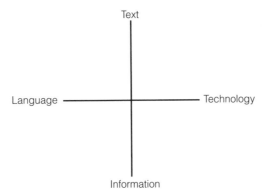

language, literacy and learning than the shunting of information'. It is not for nothing that we find some teachers, who share such values, seeking refuge in literary hypertext and the like: finding ways in which to use new applications such as hypertext to maintain familiar practices with the support of the literacy theories they are committed to. More generally, the privileging of information is highly problematic for literacy teachers—Smith-like or otherwise—who are committed to ideals such as a three-dimensional, sociocultural view of literacy as outlined here.

As much as we might sympathise with Smith's preference, we live and work in times that are, above all else, technologically textured and media-saturated: we live and work in times that are 'informationalised'. It is necessary in education to confront the ideologies and rhetorics of information. We need to develop concepts of, and approaches to, literacy education that take seriously the sociocultural nature of teaching and learning, yet which remain sensitive to the likelihood that these practices are necessarily transformed in a society that increasingly privileges information. In responding to this challenge, two key ideas advanced in this chapter provide a useful starting point. First, we need to think of literacy in terms of technology—as always-already technologised under one or more 'regimes', such as the print apparatus or the digital-electronic apparatus. Second, we need to think of literacy in terms of the relationship of text to information (see Figure 3).

It is also useful, in the context of the rapidly escalating uptake of communication and information technologies, to have some way of classifying various types of literacy-computing/computing-

Figure 4   Classification schema for computing

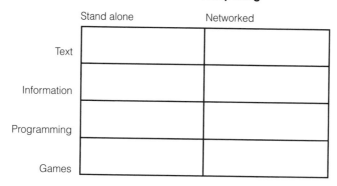

literacy. As a starting place, we suggest thinking in terms of a literacy/computing classification schema with four elements:

1 *text*-based (or -oriented) computing/software (for example, word processing, desktop publishing);
2 *information*-based (or -oriented) computing/software (for example, database, spreadsheet);
3 *programming*-based computing/software (for example, LOGO);
4 *games*-based (or -oriented) computing/software (for example, SuperMario Brothers, Myst, Where . . . is Carmen Sandiego?).

This schema provides us with an initial basis for considering the range of literate practices we need to recognise under current conditions, and their legitimacy for any comprehensive approach to literacy education. A further matter to consider here is the notion of a shift from 'stand alone' to 'networked' computing (Turkle 1995). Historically, this is how the field has developed. The development may usefully be thought of in terms of an augmentary shift from 'information' to 'communication and information' technology. Figure 4 provides a visual representation of the combinations of these different types of computing (text, information, programming, games) and the two key dimensions (stand-alone, networked).

Of course, this is only a provisional and historically contingent framework. It should not be taken as a definitive account of hard and fast distinctions and categorisations. Once people begin working with it and with different technologies as they become available (for example, virtual reality technologies), various overlaps become obvious. Hypertext/hypermedia and the internet are especially interesting to consider in terms of where and how well they fit around such classifications. The point of the schema, however, is to provide a useful starting point—particularly, one that can serve teachers. The classifications offered here are advanced with that in mind. More important than the actual schema, we believe, is the readiness to think about the changing world of literacy-technology in informed and systematic ways. Any such models and classification schemas are products of just that kind of readiness. This entire chapter can be seen as a call to develop this readiness, as effective literacy education increasingly demands it.

LEARNING

From the sociocultural perspective we are advocating in this chapter, learning is about becoming proficient participants in social practices. One of the most promising developments in learning theory in recent years has been the emergence of a 'situated social practice' model, associated with people like Barbara Rogoff (1984, 1990) and Jean Lave (Lave & Wenger 1991) among many others, and derived in significant part from the pioneering work of Lev Vygotsky (1962) and his colleagues. This model emphasises situated learning in 'authentic' contexts through processes like 'cultural apprenticeship', 'guided participation' and 'participatory appropriation' (Rogoff 1995), involving people with different degrees of experience engaging with each other, and moving through cycles of teaching, learning and practice. Within 'authentic' settings of culturally valued activity— worthwhile things to be learned—participants learn from each other, are guided by social and cultural values as well as by social partners, and improve their expertise by such means as explaining to and guiding others and by sheer practice of 'doing'.

In their account of what an 'authentic' classroom curriculum might look like, Shirley Brice Heath and Milbrey McLaughlin (1994: 472) criticise classroom pedagogies which 'create "authenticity" artificially rather than study contextually authentic curricula—authentic to youth—supportive organizational structures'. They argue that classroom teachers can learn much from examining effective grassroots organisations like the Girl Guides, girls' clubs and drama groups. These provide rich social contexts and opportunities for learning to learn 'for anything everyday' by means of '[cognitive and social] apprenticeship, peer learning, authentic tasks, skill-focused practices and real outcome measures', such as completed public projects, performances, displays and exhibitions (1994: 472).

Getting 'on the inside' of a practice and becoming expert in this way involves an appropriate balance between 'acquisition' and 'learning', as defined by James Gee. Becoming proficient participants in a social practice typically involves some mix of acquisition and learning, although the mix varies from case to case. Gee (1996: 138) defines acquisition and learning as follows:

> *Acquisition* is a process of acquiring something (usually, subconsciously) by exposure to models, a process of trial and error, and practice within social groups, without formal teaching. It happens in natural settings which are meaningful and functional in the sense that acquirers know that they need to acquire the thing they are exposed to in order to function and they in fact want to so function. This is how people come to control their first language.
>
> *Learning* is a process that involves conscious knowledge gained through teaching (though not necessarily from someone officially designated a teacher) or through certain life-experiences that trigger conscious reflection. This teaching or reflection involves explanation and analysis, that is, breaking down the thing to be learned into its analytic parts.

Acquisition and learning are good for different aspects of proficiency in a social practice. Acquisition is good for fluent performance or full proficiency. Learning is good for promoting knowledge of the practice, for understanding what it is that one is doing. There is an important point to be made here, which will lead us directly to the idea that good-quality learning involves the same three dimensions we identified for effective literacy. The point is that although we become fluent in a social practice through acquisition rather than learning, unless there is also a learning dimension (in Gee's sense) we will merely be socialised, or what Gee calls 'indoctrinated', into received ways of doing things. 'Learning' is essential if the cultural and critical dimensions of social practice are to be realised—which is what we are advocating here. Therefore, while teaching for 'acquisition' precedes and has priority over teaching for 'learning' in Gee's sense, 'learning' is crucial if cultural apprenticeship is to be appropriately balanced by cultural criticism and truly active participation. In other words, whatever the social practice might be, being educated—as opposed to being merely socialised or indoctrinated—in that social practice necessarily involves becoming competent with each of the operational, cultural and critical dimensions of the practice and the manner in which they intermesh.

There is one more feature of a sociocultural view of learning that is noteworthy before we pull together the threads of this chapter: from a sociocultural perspective, learning focuses not on children or schools, but on human lives seen as trajectories through numerous social practices across a range of social institutions. For learning to be efficacious, what a person does now as a 'learner' must be connected in meaningful and motivating ways with 'mature' versions of related social practices as practised by 'insiders' (Gee, Hull & Lankshear 1996: 4). Schools are typically not ideal settings for efficacious learning in this sense. Partly this is because they focus on children rather than on social practices, and build activities around notions of who and what children are, what their needs are and what they are presumed to be capable of doing now. Partly it is because schools are cut off from the real world of 'mature' versions of social practices. Schools create their own versions of social practices, which are often very different from 'mature' versions of the social practices to which they are supposedly related. The examples are endless: woodwork as to carpentry; newspaper stories (in columns) as to journalism; subject History as to being an historian. Schools not only separate learning from participation in 'mature' versions of social practices: to a large extent they actually mystify the connections. School-based learning becomes learning for the sake of school rather than with a view to ensuring that what is done now connects with 'authentic' social practice at later points in life trajectories.

The challenge for teachers lies in making schools and class-rooms, as much as possible, into 'worldly', socially meaningful and relevant places, characterised by what Jo-Anne Reid (1997: 150) has described as 'generic practice'—'the engaged production of social texts for real purposes'. This is crucial as we come to understand that social practices depend on what we encounter in the way of social practices—wherever and whenever we encounter them.

LITERACY, TECHNOLOGY AND LEARNING: A 3D APPROACH

In the light of what has been said, we need to strive for a 3D approach to literacy education involving new technologies: an approach that brings together the operational, cultural and critical dimensions of learning and social practice. We should not focus solely on 'how-to' knowledge, understood as technical competence and 'functional literacy'. Instead, we need pedagogies that complement and supplement such knowledge by contextualising it in ways that pay due attention to matters of culture, history and power and recognise that it is counterproductive to start with issues of 'skill' or 'technique', outside an 'authentic' context of situated social practice.

When we are thinking of the 'operational' dimension of literacy education involving new technologies, we need to attend to how to operate the language system as well as how to operate the technology system. With respect to the language system, this involves learning how to make it work for individuals' own meaning-making purposes—how to 'turn it on'. In the case of written language, for instance, the operational dimension involves understanding how the alphabet works, and recognising the letters and subsequent formulations and conventions. It also involves learning the mechanics of handwriting and keyboarding. With respect to the technology system, it involves learning how to make a computer operational, how to 'turn it on' and make it 'work': from the basics of making sure the cables are connected and switching it on, to opening up files and documents, along with related activities such as searching a database or using a CD-ROM.

Understanding and being able to draw on the 'cultural' dimension of literacy involves realising that the ability to operate language and technology systems is always in the service of participating in 'authentic' forms of social practice and meaning. We always use texts and technologies to do things in the world, and to achieve our own and others' purposes, whether in the context of school, work or everyday life. This means putting the emphasis on 'authentic' contexts, forms and purposes of learning along the axes of literacy and technology and text and information. It means building on well-informed understandings of 'mature' versions of social practice in each of the main types of literacy/computing—text-based, information-based, programming-based, games-based—as well as across stand-alone and networked applications.

Learners should not have to endure forms of literacy–technology learning that lack meaningful and motivating links to insider versions of social practices involving production, distribution and exchange of texts and information, using new technologies. To maximise insider practices in their classrooms, teachers need to avoid the 'old wine in new bottles' syndrome (Lankshear & Bigum, in press), where teachers—often under the constraint of syllabus guidelines, curriculum statements and profiles, and assessment requirements—adopt applications of new technology that mesh with familiar pedagogical styles and fit new technologies into classroom business as usual. Such approaches become problematic when long-standing language and literacy education routines, repackaged as PowerPoint slide shows and webpage presentations, become legitimised as 'authentic'. At times, this may amount to little more than teachers and students gaining opportunities to learn how to better use new technologies. That is to say, if teachers and students use these software applications in routine school literacy practices for long enough, they may well become proficient in the technical aspects. They may also, however, become cut off from more expansive and efficacious practices involving these same software applications. In the case of learners, many of whom will have access outside the classroom to more diverse and challenging practices, the outcomes of classroom activity may include boredom and confusion ('Is that what this stuff is about?'). Integrating the 3D model into classroom and school life involves prioritising in practice the cultural dimension, linking learning as closely as possible to the service of 'real-life' and 'lifelike' social practices, within consciously developed communities of practice.

The 'critical' dimension means that teachers and students need to be able to assess and evaluate software and other technology resources (databases, interactive CD-ROMs, the World Wide Web) in a spirit of informed scepticism (Durrant & Green 1998). That is, they need the ability not only to use such resources and to participate effectively and creatively in their associated cultures, but also to critique them, to read and use them against the grain, to appropriate and even redesign them, as well as to be able to actively envisage and contribute to transforming social practices as they judge appropriate.

So far as the professional roles, identities and status of literacy teachers are concerned, such a view of learning and teaching has real value. It puts education firmly in the foreground, which means emphasising literacy and curriculum issues rather than technology or technical issues. Integral to our argument in this chapter is the understanding that new technologies—any technologies—should be seen as *supporting* learning and teaching. Learning and teaching always remain 'the main game'. To this end, teachers' educational expertise needs to be strengthened, together with their professional knowledge, skills and dispositions. Teachers can then bring their wisdom to bear on the challenge new technologies pose for literacy education as well as for learning more generally.

Of course, what teachers can do in classrooms with technologies (new or old), so far as literacy education and approaches to learning in general are concerned, is far from being an open choice. Curriculum and pedagogy in practice are guided by and accountable to policy directions emanating from federal and state governments. They are also inevitably influenced by ideas, views, debates and issues that circulate publicly on the education policy scene. In chapter 3 we look at some typical examples of recent and current policy statements, as well as texts generated in the context of education policy development. We look at these in relation to the policy roles of teachers and the current challenge facing teachers to integrate new technologies into classroom learning.

3 Literacy and technology policy: why it counts and what we can learn from it

AN ORIENTING TALE

In 1996 a document called 'The national policy on literacy' surfaced in university education faculties, state education departments, the offices of teachers' professional associations and school staff rooms. It was written by Joseph Lo Bianco, then chief executive of Language Australia, and Peter Freebody, a professor in literacy education at Griffith University. Unlike many literacy policy documents, this one explicitly recognised the uses and significance of the new technologies in literacy education. In addition, more than previous policy documents, it recognised—without using the exact language—that literacy has operational, cultural and critical dimensions. As it happened, 'The national policy on literacy' never became what its name connoted: it did not receive the imprimatur of official policy. It was eventually published in 1997 as the book *Australian Literacies* (Lo Bianco & Freebody 1997).

Some morals of the tale

Not surprisingly, the document was circulating in a context that contained various other developments in the literacy field. These included a national literacy survey, literacy testing, and literacy benchmarking procedures. As part of the unfolding 'national literacy plan', commonwealth, state and territory ministers agreed to a national literacy goal that 'every child leaving primary school should be numerate and be able to read, write and spell at an appropriate level' (DEETYA 1998: 9). They also agreed to a subsidiary goal that 'every child commencing school from 1998 will achieve a minimum acceptable literacy and numeracy standard within four years' (1998: 9). The new emphasis in the national plan on the development of 'foundational literacy' (1998: 9) skills for students in the early years and 'early intervention' (1998: 10) for at-risk students is considerably narrower than that of its predecessor, the *Australian Language and Literacy Policy* (DEET 1991a, 1991b). The same contraction of focus is evident in many recent policy trends at state level.

The case of 'The national policy on literacy' provides valuable insight into the policy environment and its relevance to the day-to-day work of teachers in classrooms. It highlights the fact that when we talk about policy, we are inevitably referring to more than just the content of officially mandated policy documents. National policy on literacy education does not materialise from nowhere: 'There is always a prior history of significant events, a particular ideological and political climate, a social and economic context— and often, particular individuals as well—which together influence the shape and timing of policies as well as their evolution and outcomes', (Taylor et al. 1997: 16). The document's history also provides preliminary insight into the national literacy policy scene, where the focus is currently on standards, testing, benchmarking and reporting. In short, the tide of official policy-making for literacy was starting to flow very strongly in a different direction from that advocated in 'The national policy on literacy'. Whatever the document's original status may have been in relation to official policy development, its content was destined to be strictly marginal to ensuing federal literacy policy.

This chapter identifies what we see as some of the main literacy, technology and learning policy problems and tasks that need to be negotiated by schools and literacy teachers and dealt with at the school level. The position we are arguing for means that teachers must look for ways to develop policies at the school level that can guide them in implementing requirements like those embodied in the national literacy plan. At the same time, they must look for ways that retain and promote more expansive ideas—such as those espoused in Lo Bianco and Freebody's vision of a national literacy policy and, indeed, by the 3D model of effective literacy.

To do this, teachers need to scrutinise current policy, make informed decisions about its uptake, and engage in the important business of formulating their own policy at a local level. When, for example, teachers in Queensland read about current initiatives of Education Queensland in its recent publication, *Schooling 2001* (Education Queensland 1997), they need helpful frames of reference to decide how best to make these initiatives useful for the literacy classroom. Similarly, when teachers in Victoria access the education department's SOFWeb site (Department of Education, Victoria 1999) and encounter *Learning Technologies in Victorian Schools 1998–2001*, or read the document in glossy hard copy (Department of Education, Victoria 1998a), they need some understanding of the material and cultural conditions under which the policy was produced. They may then approach it with a keen analytical and interpretive eye.

Four ideas that inform this chapter

What we have to say builds on four core ideas, which are closely related. The first is the idea of 'relevant policy texts' in relation to the literacy–technology–learning interface. The second is the idea of the various 'policy roles' to be performed by literacy teachers. The third is the relationship between 'policy as officially formulated' and 'policy as implemented in practice'. The fourth is the idea that we need always to keep a larger picture in mind when we consider policies at national, state and local levels. We now sketch these ideas briefly in turn.

First, it is important that we do not limit our notion of policy texts to the category of official policy documents issued by governments. Policy development takes place in an arena, and many texts are produced and circulated within this arena—such as the one by Lo Bianco and Freebody (1997). Indeed, governments often call for policy submissions, or commission discussion documents intended to stimulate policy debate. Even where they do not, individuals, interest groups and organisations 'inject' statements into the policy arena with a view to getting their values and ideas represented in official policy—which inevitably highlight some positions and render others more marginal. Consequently, if teachers are to understand official policy and to implement it richly and effectively, they need to be aware of what is at stake in the policy arena. It means considering not just 'official policy texts' but, more broadly, 'relevant policy texts'—texts, connected to the policy in question, that are circulating or have circulated in that policy arena.

This brings us to the second idea. In a democratic society,

teachers have a range of legitimate roles in relation to policy development and implementation. As citizens and as members of recognised interest groups, represented by associations, teachers have a right to participate in setting policy directions by getting their ideas and values into the arena, or by lending their support to policy positions they endorse. Hence, they have a role as policy 'protagonists'. They also have roles as policy analysts and policy critics. Once policy directions begin to firm up, it is important for teachers to analyse these positions and engage critically with them. They need to understand them as clearly as possible for what they are and to assess and comment on them in appropriate contexts (such as staff meetings, meetings of their association branches, policy conferences, public forums like parents and citizens gatherings, as well as editorial and letter pages of newspapers).

Even when policies become official, teachers have multiple roles. They are required to implement policy at the level of classroom practice, but before policy can be implemented it needs to be interpreted and translated to meet the requirements of the local context. Policy statements are inevitably general and broad-brush; they cannot trade in detail, otherwise they lose their audience. Once they have been formulated, policies have to be 'turned into' practice, and there are various levels of interpretation and translation that occur before we reach the chalkface. At the school level, to avoid leaving teachers to either sink or swim, decision-makers need to determine what that policy means in their context, how it can be programmed and, given scarcity of resources, what order of priority can be given to different policy emphases.

These acts of interpretation and translation cannot be done in a vacuum. If they are to be informed and responsive in democratic terms, teachers need to know about the range and types of legitimate interests that are at stake and how to take account of them fully and equitably. Further, as education policy is dynamic rather than static—it is not set in stone—teachers have a function in keeping the policy arena alive and accountable. They have roles, then, as policy 'refiners' and policy 'activists'. That is to say, with a policy in place and the outcomes of its particular implementations becoming apparent, teachers enter another round of policy 'protagonism', policy 'analysis' and 'evaluation', policy 'critique', policy 'refining' and policy 'implementation'. Unless teachers assume these roles, policy directions and formulations become the preserve of politicians, business and commercial interests, lobbyists and pressure groups. While these policy agents have their rights within democratic policy-making processes, they do not have the right—individually or collectively—any more than teachers do, to monopolise the process.

Third, as implied in what has already been said, we need to recognise that educational practice is never a direct, simple and seamless 'realisation' of education policy. A complex chain of processes, components and agents exists between the act of formulating policy at official levels and the myriad acts of implementing policy in the classroom. To date, policy-makers at the centre have left the roles of policy interpretation, translation and implementation largely up to teachers and the institutions they work in. Increasingly, however, policy constrains the range of possible interpretations by specifying such things as benchmarks, reporting instruments and procedures.

Fourth, in our attempts to interpret and implement policy, we need to understand the Australian policy environment in a much larger global policy context. This is a context that emphasises—if not fetishises—the importance of communication and information technologies in education. Some commentators go so far as to claim that 'the whole task set by contemporary education policy is to keep up with rapidly shifting developments in technology' (Aronowitz & Giroux 1993: 63).

President Clinton's 'Technology Literacy Challenge' policy package of February 1996 has set the tone and pace for many initiatives across the West and beyond. Aimed at ensuring that all students are 'technologically literate' by 'the dawn of the 21st century', it defines 'technological literacy' as 'computer skills and the ability to use computers and other technology to improve learning, productivity and performance', and claims that this new literacy 'has become as fundamental to a person's ability to navigate through society as traditional skills like reading, writing and arithmetic' (US Department of Education 1996: 5).

The policy is an overt response to claims, like that of the US National Science Board, that 'alarming numbers of young Americans are ill-equipped to work in, contribute to, profit from, and enjoy our increasingly technological society'. Its strategy is to ensure that all teachers receive the necessary training and support to 'help students learn via computers and the information superhighway'; to develop 'effective and engaging software and on-line learning resources' as integral elements of school curricula; to provide all teachers and students with access to modern computers; and to connect every US classroom to the internet (Winters 1996). As will become apparent when we turn to examples of key Australian policies, parallel emphases and constructions of 'technological literacy for the millennium' can readily be found in the Australian context, and what is happening in Australia closely parallels global trends, even down to the rhetoric employed by governments to persuade teachers to 'get technologised'.

More generally, as in other countries, education policy initiatives in Australia are being developed within material and cultural conditions of a rapidly changing world—a world characterised by the rise of the information age, the decline of national sovereignty, the loss of governmental influence, community disorientation at the pace of change, disillusionment with politics, the blurring of boundaries between politics, education and entertainment. It is also a more deregulated world, driven by market considerations, in which people are expected to be more self-sufficient and, it is said, need to be 'smarter'; where 'equity' and 'access' and 'being enterprising' are espoused; where tasks are devolved. This is the global world order towards which contemporary education policy initiatives seek to steer us. Becoming clearer about worldwide patterns and directions of change, and pressures to run with that change, is an important aspect of professionally relevant knowledge. It is essential for informing the kind of objectivity and distance from policy enthusiasms and exhortations that allow us to keep our pedagogical priorities focused on educational ends, and to avoid getting swept away by 'hyped-up texts' about technology's inevitable contribution to educational advance.

The structure of the rest of the chapter

The remainder of the chapter is arranged in five sections, beginning with an account of 'policy', where we describe its purposes and functions, how it 'works' in the world, and its relevance to teachers. The next section presents an overview of salient points arising from the original project survey of the national literacy, technology and learning policy environment. This is followed by a parallel overview of the literacy, technology and learning policy environments in two states—Queensland and Victoria. The *Digital Rhetorics* report (Digital Rhetorics 1999; Lankshear et al. 1997) also examined state-level policy development in New South Wales, but shortage of space precludes our dealing with those policies here. Clearly, teachers in Queensland have to negotiate their way around a somewhat different kind of 'policy reality' from teachers in Victoria, and there are further variations in the other states and territories. Nonetheless, we can learn some important things from these two cases: in their own right, and as descriptions that enable readers from other places to decide the extent to which the situation in either Queensland or Victoria is similar to, and thus likely to be instructive about, their own. In the fourth section we distil some of the key issues, tasks and challenges teachers have to consider in their attempts to navigate the national and state policy environments on the way to developing effective school programs. We conclude with a brief account of how one school has responded strategically to the challenge of developing effective policies to guide classroom practice by approaching policy development as an integrated exercise across literacy, technology and the 'key learning areas'.

UNDERSTANDING POLICY

What is policy? Policy can be defined quite simply as plans of action made by organisations. In our analysis of the Australian policy scene we are interested in two main kinds of policy: the first are public policies, made on behalf of the state, to steer the conduct of individuals (for example, teachers and students) and of organisations (for example, schools); the second are local practices in policy formation, initiated by smaller units such as schools, to guide the professional activities of the people that work in them. We look at both public and local educational policies here, ranging from national policies, through those developed by state departments of education, to those produced in schools by administrators, teachers and parents.

What is policy for? According to Taylor et al. (1997), public policies in education have three main functions: to provide an account of the cultural norms considered by the state as desirable in education; to institute a mechanism of accountability against which student and teacher performance can be measured; and to manage public calls for change, giving them form and direction. This last point about the connection between policy formation and change is of particular relevance to our concerns, which should not be construed as simply literacy, technology and learning but more accurately as literacy, technology, learning and change. Clearly, the emergence of new technologies has already altered dramatically the patterns of everyday life, restructured work and leisure, and now demands revisions to educational policy, especially to curriculum priorities and pedagogical approaches.

How is policy best understood? The conventional view is that policy constitutes an informed statement of principles and recommendations that are intended to shape, guide and direct practice. Such a view is consistent with a common understanding of the relationship between theory and practice: that theory serves to inform and structure practice. However, we think that this explanation of the relationship between policy and practice, sometimes called the rational model, is oversimplified: it gives the impression that policies are implemented in straightforward and unproblematic ways. We see policy as something that is struggled over at all stages by competing interests. Hence, policy rarely comes out in practice in exactly the way it is promulgated. In part, this can be explained by resistance—an unwillingness by the target audience to take up the policy directions as prescribed. But there are other reasons, not least inconsistencies between different levels of policy-making and policy-policing. There are contradictions, gaps and fissures, but also, we are keen to point out, opportunities for 'creative' responses. These opportunities may be realised as subversive actions of some sort, or at least provide the possibility of achieving outcomes neither intended nor predicted by the policy-makers.

Rather than a one-way, top-down movement from policy to practice, as described in the rational model, policy and practice are mutually conditioning and directly interrelated. In this view, policy is as much a form of practice as practice is a form of policy; most importantly, teachers and other school personnel are directly implicated and engaged in the making and remaking of policy. Policy-making may take the form of school-level, subject-department or even classroom policy work. Policy is not just something that is done by 'them' for 'us' to implement; rather it is part of teachers' everyday work.

Policy can also be understood as symbolic action: that is, as 'a way of shaping public consciousness and giv[ing] meaning and direction to an entire sphere of social relations and social institutions' (Kliebard 1992: 184). In this sense, the main function of policy as symbolic action will reside in 'its use of language to organise allegiances, perceptions and attitudes' (1992: 185). Consequently, policy is concerned not only with trying to shape more or less directly what people do and how institutions function in the world; policy is concerned also with influencing how people understand and experience the world within institutional contexts—for example, trying to mobilise teachers behind the 'need' to 'technologise' learning in classrooms. We can view the Lo Bianco and Freebody document as an exercise in policy as symbolic action, as in the context of a narrowing policy conception of literacy their statement lobbied for our allegiance to a more expansive view.

Below we focus on a range of 'official' policy documents. The dual role of policy, however, means that when we work at the school level to frame policies and plans in order to interpret and implement national and state-level requirements we must, and almost inevitably will, attend to more than just the actual policy documents and mandates of governments. We also attend to unofficial, informal policy statements, such as discussion or position papers and commissioned reports, which exist and have influence in the public domain but have not been legislated or otherwise officially approved.

As we have already indicated, the relationship between policy and practice is ambiguous. We know that change in practice can and often does occur regardless of policy interventions—likewise, that in many cases policy interventions result in little or no change (Taylor et al. 1997). So why does policy matter at all? We believe that becoming informed about the policy process is an important part of educational agency. This includes understanding policy as the authoritative allocation of resources and values, but also that policy formation is never unproblematic or uncontested. It means grasping the notion of policy having a significant impression-management function. In a complex and volatile political environment, it is not so much that things need to be done but that they need to be seen to be done; policy becomes a matter of image.

Notwithstanding, it would be unwise to dismiss altogether the 'steering' function of policy—the notion that, although policy does not and indeed cannot determine educational practice, it may be seen as informing and guiding it—and is certainly formulated at official levels with a view to doing precisely that. We argue that both the material and the symbolic dimensions of policy must be attended to in our assessment of literacy, technology and educational policy and practice.

Finally, as already suggested, policy should not be seen as the exclusive domain of governments or systems. Schools as organisations and classroom teachers as individuals need to see themselves as makers of policy, not only in the informal sense but as the creators of official documents. In this way, it is possible to see policy operating at a number of different levels, each in dialogue and negotiation with each other but still maintaining a degree of uniqueness. To realise their policy-making function most effectively, schools need to draw on informed understanding of the wider policy context.

THE LITERACY, TECHNOLOGY AND LEARNING POLICY ENVIRONMENT

Here we consider the public policy environment in relation to literacy, technology and learning. Concentrating on the period from the mid-1980s, when educational interest in information technology began to develop on a significant scale, to the present, we look at the national scene and then at two states, Queensland and Victoria. We suggest how the sociocultural framework, developed in chapter 2, can be used to interpret and assess the policies included in our survey.

The national scene

In our overview of examples of two groups of policy texts at the national level, the first group focuses broadly on technology, culture and learning, while the second deals directly with 'literacy' and 'technology' but as discrete areas. We look here at the 'national literacy plan', referred to earlier, which is now the official Australian literacy policy. At this time there is still no national numeracy plan or national technology plan, despite federal government intentions.

Group one: national policy texts pertaining to technology, culture and learning
Although only one of the selected policy documents in this group refers directly to literacy as such, collectively they provide a strong sense of the cultural importance attributed to new technologies in recent times. They contribute to shaping a view of the world that needs to be taken into account by education in general, and by literacy education in particular. The first document to be considered is *Australia as an Information Society* (Parliament of Commonwealth of Australia 1991). This document can be seen retrospectively as ushering in an overdue consideration of the 'information society' and its implications for Australia. Information is portrayed as an economic commodity, but the broader role of information in an educated society is also acknowledged.

The report recommends that 'national information policy' should take into account the 'disparity between the "information rich" and the "information poor"' (1991: 20). This entails an educational obligation to take heed of access and equity issues as well as other dimensions of educational policy and practice. The document identifies 'a need for people to develop information awareness and skills in a more concerted way than is currently the case in education' (1991: 26). While it places the responsibility more directly on the tertiary sector than on schools to achieve this objective, it lays a basis for subsequent initiatives in the school sector. The use of information—not its mere accumulation—is emphasised, as is the importance of distinguishing between 'information' and 'knowledge'.

The convergence of work and learning emerges as a key focus in the second document, *Young People's Participation in Post-Compulsory Education and Training* (Australian Education Council 1991). Indeed, 'convergence' can be seen as an emerging theme in this group of policy documents more generally. The emphasis in this report, as in many other policy statements in the public policy arena, is on 'skills and knowledge-based' competencies (1991: xvii).

The theme of convergence is also taken up in *Converging Technology, Work and Learning* (NBEET 1995). According to this document, education must equip the workforce and the community with the skills necessary to exploit technological development. Technocultural change is seen as having 'profound implications for the way people work, interact, educate and entertain themselves in the future' (NBEET 1995: 4).

The policy perspective here implies a need for schools and teachers to take seriously the connections between school and the world beyond when constructing school-based policies. More specifically, the document implies that school practices need to be in touch with new literacy practices, and not merely 'skills' associated with the use of new technologies in workplaces, businesses, homes and recreation spaces. When we bring a sociocultural perspective to the policy position under review here, we conclude (Lankshear 1998: 55–6):

> If learners are to acquire effective technological literacies and learn how to use new technologies proficiently, they need access to purposeful contexts and applications. Teachers need to have a sense of what these are, how to get them into the classroom and, where necessary, how to get the classroom to them.

The third document, *Creative Nation* (Commonwealth of Australia 1994), highlights the role and significance of culture, which is defined as 'encompass[ing] our entire mode of life, our ethics, our institutions, our manners and our routines, not only interpreting our world but shaping it'. Australian culture is described as 'an exotic hybrid', flourishing not just because of the increasingly multicultural orientation of the population, but more specifically and increasingly because of the 'global awareness created by the electronic media' (1994: 1).

Concerned with the threat to Australian culture presented by the IT revolution and the wave of global mass culture, *Creative Nation* advocates confronting the information revolution and the new media 'not with fear and loathing, but with imagination and wit' (1994: 7). It emphasises an expansive arts and cultural education system that invokes a comprehensive range of educational values, including creativity as well as skills, making for a stark contrast with the narrow focus of the national literacy plan. Although links between literacy, technology and learning are never made explicit, there are implications in the document's propositions for the aesthetic and cultural dimensions of literacy and technology education. Teachers might even consider including phrases such as 'with imagination and wit' in a school policy document as a source of inspiration when making decisions about how best to integrate new technologies into curriculum practices.

The final document to be considered in this group is *Education and Technology Convergence* (Tinkler, Lepani & Mitchell 1996). This is one of a very few we surveyed that makes useful connections between literacy, technology and learning. Acknowledging the expansion of global communication networks, it argues for the need to 'look beyond "computer literacy" and consider the importance of "information literacy" which takes into account the development of higher-order skills in processing information' (Tinkler et al. 1996: x). The document identifies several key issues that need to be taken into account by teachers engaged in policy formation at the local level:

- resource people to provide technical and human support;
- effective leadership;
- adequate and appropriate professional development;
- incentives to encourage teachers to use information technologies;
- the increasingly important role of librarians and libraries;
- the problem of inbuilt obsolescence;
- the costs involved—infrastructure, hardware, software, upgrading, maintenance, technical support and professional development.

Schools are described as 'evolving learning communities', built increasingly around networked links to homes, community learners and local businesses, as well as to university, Technical and Further Education (TAFE) and international education sites. New media forms and technological trends are recognised and their implications for education and other institutions highlighted. Emphasis is given to the prospect of important changes to literacy practices—in particular, those associated with the use of multimedia. In the view of Tinkler et al., teachers must become as competent in the use and production of the new media as they have traditionally been in reading and writing. The convergent technologies can support a shift in emphasis from teaching to learning, and identify different types of learning in a new knowledge-economy framework. Drawing on ideas from commentators such as Peter Drucker (1993), the authors claim that, within attempts to reshape schools and to challenge received forms of education, technology will be important primarily because it encourages and compels us to 'do new things rather than enable us to do old things better' (Tinkler et al. 1996: 97).

In chapter 1 we claimed that the literacy activities in the three schools we described were, to a large extent, predictable and school-like. Students used new technologies to do more or less what they had always done. Statements like *Education and Technology Convergence* insist that this need not be the case and advocate that it not be the case. They offer teachers and schools wider views of how school learning, mediated by the use of the new technologies, could be. Tinkler et al. (1996) make many concrete suggestions about the ways in which new kinds of learning contexts may be achieved that could be of immediate use to teachers responsible for literacy, technology and learning policy formation in schools.

While *Education and Technology Convergence* tackles the theme most explicitly and at greatest length, it is fair to say that this group of policy documents as a whole highlights learning, which it links directly to notions of information and technology and, more specifically, to literacy and computing. Although the emphasis remains on cultural and economic change in the context of information and knowledge, these documents advocate a reorientation towards a learning-based society and, by implication, towards a learning-based approach to formal education. Unfortunately for school policy developers, the meaning of the term 'learning' is systematically ambiguous. It can mean as many different things as there are theories and paradigms of learning, and can apply as narrowly as to rote learning a dictum or becoming adept at a simple skill, or as widely as to learning an entire social practice, taking account of its operational, cultural and critical dimensions. Schools need to decide where they stand on such matters if they are to develop coherent policies around a call to 'learning'.

Group two: national policy texts pertaining to literacy and technology

The policy documents in this second group deal directly with 'literacy' and 'technology' as discrete Key Learning Areas. Our survey of these documents suggests that it was not until the mid-1990s that attention was focused on the importance of 'technoliteracies'.

The *Australian Language and Literacy Policy* (ALLP) (DEET 1991a, 1991b) emerged after a long period of debate on literacy and schooling, which first gathered momentum in the 1970s (Green, Hodgens & Luke 1994). The policy asserts that basic literacy is no longer sufficient for effective participation in modern society: more sophisticated, abstract capacities are required than were needed in the past. Language and literacy are described as 'central to the reshaping and the improved performances of our education and training systems' (DEET 1991a: 1). 'Effective literacy' is the literacy baseline for Australians, defined as 'intrinsically purposeful, flexible and dynamic and involv[ing] the integration of speaking, listening, and critical thinking with reading and writing' (1991a: 5). Literacy is thus constructed as a combination of 'critical thinking'—'a generic grab bag for higher order skills of comprehension, problem-solving and analysis—and reading, writing, speaking and listening' (Lankshear 1998: 48).

Significantly, the ALLP presents an official view of literacy that is more or less exclusively print-oriented, without recognising that this in itself represents a particular relationship between language and technology, namely the printing press and the publishing industry. Libraries and the media are mentioned, but are not seen as directly relevant to literacy policy. The ALLP was not on its own in this respect. The *Teaching English Literacy* report, which focuses on the preservice preparation of English literacy teachers, was published in the same year (Christie et al. 1991). Like the ALLP, this report gives little recognition to the literacy challenges associated with new technologies and technocultural change. While formally commissioned as a 'Project of National Significance', the report was never formally endorsed by government.

The Literacy Challenge (Parliament of Commonwealth of Australia 1992) calls for 'a nation dedicated to universal literacy', with the aim that 'every Australian must be able to read and write in English' (1992: vii). This document set the stage for a return to a narrower focus on basic literacy within a year of the ALLP being released. The recommendations were to be accompanied by new funding arrangements, but these did not eventuate until 1998—and under a different government—when the Coalition's commitment to universal functional literacy by Year 4 was fully endorsed. The emphasis of *The Literacy Challenge* is firmly and exclusively on print literacy. Interestingly, for a document expressly concerned with the early school years, no account is taken of the emergence during the 1980s and 90s of a distinctive 'Nintendo' culture, organised around computer and video games, or of the significance for children of television and other forms of media culture.

As part of the National Curriculum project, 'Statements and Accompanying Profiles' were published in the eight Key Learning Areas (KLAs) in 1994. Three points in particular stand out here. First, literacy and learning requirements are in no way exclusive to the English KLA. Second, the KLA statements and profiles, taken as a whole, understand literacy as being essentially verbal-linguistic in nature. We do not accept this view: rather, we endorse Nea Stewart-Dore's (1996) argument that a multimodal perspective on literacy is needed. Third, and most importantly, what characterises the entire array of KLAs is an overall commitment to print literacy. With the exception of the Technology KLA, as might be expected, literacy and learning are understood overwhelmingly in terms of language and text, with only limited and restricted reference to matters of technology and information.

When we look specifically at *A Statement on English for Australian Schools* (Curriculum Corporation 1994a) and *English—A Curriculum Profile for Australian Schools* (Curriculum Corporation 1994b), our general comments about all eight statements and profiles are confirmed. Both documents remain clearly and emphatically within the ambit of print culture and literacy. They seek to make certain connections with media and computing, consistent with their extended understanding of the notion of 'text', but print and its associated forms of literacy and rationality clearly remain the organising focus.

The 'National Plan for Literacy in Australian Schools' became the official policy in 1998, supplanting the ALLP, and requires particular attention. Key components of the plan include: assessment of all students by teachers as early as possible in their schooling; early intervention strategies for learners assessed as having difficulty with literacy learning; development of literacy 'benchmarks' for Years 3, 5, 7 and 9, against which the literacy achievement of all students will be measured; and progress towards reporting student achievement against the benchmarks (DEETYA 1998: 10). This policy replicates procedures and trends already well established in Britain and in many American states.

Close examination reveals that the national plan reflects an emphasis on what has been called 'lingering basics' (Lankshear 1998), where the notion of basic literacy as proficiency in fundamentals of encoding and decoding print texts continues to 'linger' from the 1960s and 70s. Basic literacy is framed in terms of knowing the alphabetic script visually and phonetically, and grasping the mechanism of putting elements of the script together to encode or decode words and to separate words or add them together to read and write sentences. Proposed approaches to remedial literacy work focus heavily on accuracy and self-correction in reading-aloud exercises and correct spelling in written work. In this vein, the plan recommends that at-risk learners be subjected to batteries of word recognition and dictation activities and tests as well as letter identification and print concept exercises. Teachers are required to maintain accurate and comprehensive records for diagnosis, validation, accountability and reporting purposes.

From the perspective of literacy as sociocultural practice (outlined in chapter 2), serious problems arise from the national plan with respect to implementing benchmarks. To serve the purposes of literacy in a more expansive and socially realistic sense, benchmarks would need to be framed in ways that honoured literacy as sociocultural practice; to serve as indicators of effective literacy, they would need to take account of the operational, cultural and critical dimensions of literacy. In addition, assessment would need to be of literacy in practice, otherwise benchmarking would probably end up resembling the worst examples of decontextualised assessment of competencies in workplace settings (Lankshear 1998).

With respect to the plan's emphasis on the development of 'foundational literacy' (1998: 9) skills for students in the early years, we need to ask: Foundational literacy for what? When we think about the purposes of school learning and its connections to the literacies and discourses students will need in their lives beyond school, the notion of foundational literacy embodied in the plan may well seem extremely limited and limiting. We also need to ask: Does the notion of 'foundational' literacy allow for the need to include the all-important cultural and critical understandings and knowledge, as well as the operational understandings and knowledge that go far beyond mere encoding and encoding? As with the plan's predecessor, the ALLP, any serious concern with literacies mediated by new communication and information technologies is conspicuous by its absence.

Overall, at the national level, the articulation of coherent, effective policies, informed by a sociocultural approach to literacy, the three dimensions of literacy education, and taking into account all three constructs—literacy, technology and learning—simply does not exist in landmark policy conceptions and texts. This does not mean that administrators and teachers themselves cannot move towards more integrated policies consistent with the goals of the national plan—polices that take into consideration the significance of both literacy and information technology in learning and schooling, the interconnections between them, the changing nature of literacy itself in increasingly technologised conditions, and the new and emerging cultural and curriculum practices.

The states

A major shift in emphasis on new technologies at the state level of education policy development has occurred since the mid-1980s—a shift from the mere beginnings of interest in technology matters to the high interest that characterises current and recent policy statements. The shift at the state level seems much sharper than at the national level of policy activity. Attention to 'the technological' is clearly evident in policy work currently being done in all states. In the late 1990s information technology became the hot item, with the states seemingly taking every media opportunity to parade their ideological and financial commitment to the provision of hardware and software for both students and teachers. We focus here on two states, Queensland and Victoria.

Queensland

In Queensland, policies connected with curriculum and pedagogy are overlaid by five general *Principles of Effective Learning and Teaching* (Department of Education, Queensland 1994a). These comprise a corporate ethos intended to guide policy and practice alike in all areas of a school's curricular work. The five principles state that: (i) effective learning and teaching is founded on an understanding of the learner; (ii) effective learning and teaching requires active construction of meaning; (iii) effective learning and teaching enhances and is enhanced by a supportive and challenging environment; (iv) effective learning and teaching is enhanced through worthwhile learning partnerships; and (v) effective learning and teaching shapes and responds to social and cultural contexts (1994a: 1).

These principles build on six key underlying assumptions: (i) every person is a learner; (ii) the learning process is ongoing and lifelong; (iii) people learn within social and cultural contexts, both independently and through interaction with others; (iv) what is learned depends on how and with whom it is learned; (v) key elements making for effective teaching include identifying how others learn best, extending their ways of learning, creating opportunities for learning, and evaluating outcomes of learning; and (vi) collectively, the principles provide the basis for continuing enhancement of learning and teaching practices. These assumptions support the following conceptions of 'learner', 'teacher', 'learning', and 'teaching': (i) learning involves making meaning out of experience; (ii) teaching is about guiding and facilitating this making of meaning out of experience; (iii) learners include all who are involved in the transactions around which learning occurs, as it is not pupils alone who learn in the processes involved; and (iv) teachers include students, parents, caregivers, other community members, as well as the professional teacher.

These principles can be seen as a response to well-established educational values from the past, as well as to contemporary developments in educational theory and research, informed by current positions from constructivist theory, social cognition, cognitive science and theories of inclusivity. They emphasise learning over teaching—a motif we have identified in some national-level policy documents—which accords with trends towards greater self-sufficiency and independence as widely espoused conditions of the information age (where, it is said, the short shelf-life of knowledge undermines teacher-directed, content-filled education). At the same time, the principles reflect such established educational values as inclusiveness, social justice, equality of opportunity, the importance of continuity of experience, holistic development of learners, community involvement, civic capacity and commitment, and a knowledge of past and present and how they are related.

The *English in Years 1 to 10 Queensland Syllabus* (Department of Education, Queensland 1994b) is the central curriculum policy document for literacy education. Several supplementary policies mandate initiatives, such as the *Year 2 Net* and the *Literacy and Numeracy Strategy* (Department of Education, Queensland 1995a, 1994c) with a view to enhancing literacy teaching and learning at different levels. As the policy was being ushered in, its implementation was assisted by an in-service program using the draft syllabus materials. The syllabus draws explicitly on five theoretical 'approaches' to language and literacy curriculum (Department of Education, Queensland 1994b: 1–2), described as 'cultural heritage', 'skills', 'growth, developmental, process and whole language', 'functional linguistics and genre-based', and 'critical literacy'. The hybrid package of approaches reflects the wide-ranging debate among literacy professionals and academics during the twelve-year period from 1982, when syllabus development began.

Very little explicit reference is made in the syllabus to new technologies or distinctive literacies associated with new technologies. The syllabus does, however, implicitly support and encourage teaching and learning such literacies through its emphasis on the context-text model. The relative absence of references to new technologies, and the kind of references that are made, evince the widespread tendency identified in chapter 2 to translate 'literacy' in literary rather than in social terms. The danger is that the interface between new technologies and literacy will remain constrained by literary perspectives, which will limit its educational scope and play into the hands of further 'doing business as usual' or 'doing school' (as explained in chapter 1).

In 1993 a committee chaired by Professor Ken Wiltshire reviewed the Queensland school curriculum. *Shaping the Future* (the Wiltshire Report) (Department of Education, Queensland 1994d), followed by a nine-page summary of recommendations (Department of Education, Queensland 1994e), advocated establishing a core curriculum covering the eight Key Learning Areas, revamping the upper secondary school curriculum, and creating new structures to oversee curriculum development and implementation.

These documents have many 'back-to-basics' overtones. Apart from the possibility of providing software programs for pilot projects on extension work for gifted students, the recommendations made no specific reference to new technologies. Literacy initiatives have a 'foundations' and 'skill improvement' emphasis with a subsequent increase in implementation of literacy intervention programs, like 'Reading Recovery'. Perhaps their most noteworthy features include: the invisible place they assign to new technologies; the lack of emphasis they give to the cultural and critical dimensions of literacy; and the fact that the 'back-to-basics' ethos runs against the tide of educational reform in countries like the USA, where 'excellence' has displaced 'basics' in the quest to diffuse 'higher-order' skills of problem-solving and critique as widely as possible among learners.

Queensland has also produced substantial documents relating to technology and learning: notably its *Computers in Learning Policy* (Department of Education, Queensland 1995b), *Guidelines for the Use of Computers in Learning* (Department of Education, Queensland 1995c), and *Schooling 2001* (Education Queensland 1997). The first defines learning technology and establishes departmental priorities. Learning technology is concerned with the use of computers and related technologies in learning. This focus tackles the 'educational implications of computers to enhance and extend learning and teaching' (Department of Education, Queensland 1995b: 3). Policy priorities are that: (i) students will use computers to attain curriculum goals; (ii) students will develop skills and competencies in using computers and an understanding of the role of computers in society; and (iii) teachers will acquire skills and competencies in the use and application of computers (1995b).

The *Guidelines* specify educational aims and goals for both students and teachers. The aims of computer use in class are to support and enhance the achievement of educational goals across the P–12 curriculum within a flexible, responsive and challenging learning environment. Student goals include: developing skills for using computers, developing appropriate attitudes to their use and using them for a range of purposes; understanding the role of computers in society; and being able to manage information and critically interpret and evaluate computer-mediated information. Teacher goals are to develop skills for using computers in administrative, preparation and presentation work; to incorporate computers into effective learning in ways that ensure equitable access, participation and outcomes for students; and to participate in ongoing discussion and experimentation related to the use of computers in the curriculum (Department of Education, Queensland 1995c). Explicit reference is made to the need for professional development, teacher education and support to be provided by the department in the form of systemic incentives, as well as by individual schools.

Specific themes are addressed under the headings of 'curriculum applications', 'understanding learners', 'learning and teaching processes', 'learning environments', and 'review and evaluation'. Each Key Learning Area is addressed in the curriculum applications section, offering examples of possible applications. The segment on English refers primarily to using computers for word-processing, but also mentions the possibility of critically evaluating 'the image of computers in popular culture', the importance of comprehending 'the structure of [software] texts', and 'the development of spoken language skills in the use of adventure and simulation software' (1995c: 13). We see here, again, the influence of the language/ literary paradigm prevailing over a well-developed literacy as socio-cultural phenomenon perspective.

The ways in which the department will assist schools to achieve the goals and aims of the *Computers in Learning Policy* are outlined in *Schooling 2001* (Education Queensland 1997), an initiative set in the context of 'an urgent need to move to a new educational paradigm if our schools are to be relevant in the new millennium' (1997: iii). Schools now have to deal with the I-generation, today's students who 'interact effortlessly with the new information and communications media' (1997: iii). In this context, 'we need to review the structure and organisation of the school day, the curriculum, teaching strategies and assessment practices and to identify the skills needed by teachers to operate in this new environment'. The professional development and training of teachers emerges as the major focus of the project. *Schooling 2001* is in fact a set of 'projects', described as learning technology grants, submission-based projects, and systemic initiatives. Systemic initiatives include a teacher learning technology competencies project, and all schools are expected to produce a 3–5 year plan by 1999.

Victoria

The *Curriculum and Standards Framework: English* (Board of Studies, Victoria 1995) is intended to provide the basis for curriculum planning in Victorian schools. It is part of a larger document that includes all eight KLAs. (At the time of writing, the framework was under review and a draft of the revamped version was in circulation.) Its structure derives from the 'National Statements and Profiles' (Curriculum Corporation 1994a, 1994b), and the focus is on English language learning through the study of texts—spoken, read, viewed and written—concentrating on context, purpose and audience. Language development is seen to involve three key processes: learning language, learning through language, and learning about language.

While information technology, in its various forms, is not neglected in the *Curriculum and Standards Framework*, it is fair to say that it is presented simply as another medium. This enables the emphasis to be placed on what might be called 'content' production and reception, as well as on the form of 'delivery', with the means not considered. Interestingly, several earlier documents took greater account of the importance of new technologies. The first, *English and Computers, P–12* (Ministry of Education, Victoria 1986), has as its basic premise that the computer can be a valuable tool in 'enabling students to develop and extend their abilities in using language' (1986: iii). Informed by a sociocultural approach to language learning, it offers practical guidance on ways of using computers to support classroom language programs. The second, *English Language Framework: P–10* (Ministry of Education, Victoria 1988), was designed to help schools formulate their English policies, develop their programs and devise activities. Two principles underpin the framework: to provide effective access to all students, and to recognise that language growth is a developmental process. Claims made for word processing are that it enhances writing practices and promotes valuable group discussion around evolving texts. Both documents were forward-thinking in recognising computers as effective writing machines.

Since the election of the Kennett Liberal government in 1992, the *Schools of the Future* program (Directorate of School Education, Victoria 1993) has formed the centrepiece of the policy environment. In essence, it has involved a systematic devolution of finances and management, as well as curriculum and administration more generally, in accordance with the ethos of the self-managing school. Among subsequent initiatives is the 'Classrooms of the Future' program, from which has emanated the 'Navigator Schools' program (seven schools in Victoria) and related forms of 'lighthouse' professional and curriculum development. The Smith Report, *Technologies for Enhanced Learning* (Directorate of School Education, Victoria 1994), is a key relevant document here, for until recently it provided de-facto policy guidelines for information technology in education. The Smith Report contributed significantly to popularising talk of 'learning technologies' and the notion of enhanced learning through the use of new technologies. 'Learning' features prominently as a keyword, as does 'networking'. Emphasis is placed on the notion of 'open learning' as distinct from 'distance learning', with attention to associated concepts of 'choice', 'flexibility' and 'lifelong learning'. Further, science and technology are presented as absolutely central to the reorganisation and reconceptualisation of education and schooling.

At issue is the shift of schooling in Victoria towards a generalised 'open learning' model, with IT perceived as the key to profound changes envisaged in the structure and function of schooling. The document places great store on the revolutionary and transformative implications of the new technologies for education and schooling. No statements are directed specifically to literacy and the new technologies, although a tacit concern with this theme might be read into the Smith Report—granted the assumption that literacy is fundamental to curriculum and learning and central to the technologisation of society and school. It seems more reasonable, however, to see this omission as an index of the systematic failure to understand the fundamental linkage between literacy and technology and the profound significance of literacy as a key 'learning technology'.

In 1997, *Information Technology in English* was published (Board of Studies, Victoria 1997), one of a set of eight similar charts created for each of the eight KLAs. The document summarises the connections between IT and English in terms of learning outcomes. As a recent publication, it indicates that more direct and explicit connections are now being made between the two areas. The chart suggests that IT is a powerful tool to enable students to achieve important learning outcomes. However, the emphasis is definitely on the operational dimension of literacy, with little acknowledgment of the cultural and the critical.

The current enthusiasm for technology is palpable in the recent document, *Learning Technologies in Victorian Schools 1998–2001* (Department of Education, Victoria 1998a). Its central objective is that by 2001 all schools will have implemented a 'Learning Technologies Plan' that will ensure principals, staff and students access to technology, as routine, competent and discriminating users, with a range of skills and showing leadership and innovation in the use of the technologies. On the road to 2001, schools are directed to: develop curriculum, teaching and learning strategies; improve and accelerate teachers' confidence and skills through professional development opportunities; develop an integrated and organisational plan; and identify leadership/administrative staff objectives. In addition to the learning technology plan and implementation strategy developed by each school, statewide mechanisms will be instituted to support implementation of learning technologies. These include: negotiation between general managers (schools) and principals to ensure that the objectives are reflected in the principals' professional goals; school charters to produce a clear statement on 'the role of learning technologies in the development of improved learning outcomes for students' (1998a: 24); the use of learning technologies to be a criterion for principal class selection; and learning technologies and understanding to be part of the annual review and performance management process for school staff. Getting schools up to speed with technology appears to be the number one item on the education agenda in Victoria.

Direct reference is made to the technologies' 'potential to enhance the quality of teaching and learning' (1998a: 8), essential if students are to 'operate successfully and confidently in a technologically enhanced community' (1998a: 9). The document lists the supposed benefits of using 'the new learning technologies'. For students, these include: student-centred learning; opportunities for collaboration, local and global; new roles; acquisition of knowledge, skills and attitudes essential 'for a successful and fulfilling life in the next millennium' (1998a: 10). For teachers, benefits include: a wider range of teaching strategies; opportunities to meet the needs of all students; access via the internet to resources, collegial and professional associations, and new roles; streamlined administration. For schools, these include: stimulated students, empowered teachers, partnerships with business, academic and community organisations; innovative staffing practices; team approaches. Our response to these claims is: probably only if accompanied by, at very least, a 3D understanding of literacy, technology and learning. The document also defines the challenges facing these objectives as: access/infrastructure/ resources; content development; and professional development. Continuing with the policy of devolution described in the 'Schools of the Future' policy, school-based implementation is promoted and suggestions are included about how to go about achieving the goals in a systematic way.

An accompanying statement, the *Learning Technologies Teachers' Capabilities Statement* (Department of Education, Victoria 1998b), is a resource package designed to support planning of teachers' professional development in learning technologies. It aims to enable school leaders and individual teachers to assess professional development needs and suggest programs, resources and strategies for developing skills and capabilities. The guide offers a framework against which professional development can be targeted.

These two documents, and indeed most of the documents released since the mid-1990s in Victoria, use the terms 'information technology', 'technology' and 'learning technology' somewhat loosely. The confusion created matters, as the effective response of schools and teachers depends on more or less shared and consistent understandings of what each term means. The Smith Report paved the way for these policy initiatives by familiarising Victorian teachers with the notion of 'learning technologies' and connecting its use with 'enhanced' learning and teaching. However, there has been little questioning of why it may be problematic to juxtapose the two constructs 'learning' and 'technology', nor whether 'enhanced' pedagogical opportunities for students and teachers are in fact facilitated when the technologies are used. The employment of such rhetoric represents a somewhat naive response to the possibilities but also to the problems associated with the use of new technologies (Snyder, in press). Explanations of power and the technologies of power should avoid generalising: clearly the technologies are not neutral, but neither are they wholly good or wholly evil.

Another point needs to be made. The two documents are part of the family of Victorian policy documents related to 'Schools of the Future', the model for self-governing schools. As such, they represent an explicit, top-down policy imperative in which consultation was minimal, if not non-existent. Consultative approaches, built into the process, might have elicited greater commitment for the policy prescription from the school communities they were designed for, with improved chances for their long-term survival and positive educational outcomes.

The paper versions of these documents (Department of Education, Victoria 1998a), which can also be accessed at the department's website (Department of Education, Victoria 1999), have a corporate look, content and style in the tenor of the times. The objectives are laid out, the methods of accomplishing them suggested, the required outcomes determined, and failure to conform associated with undesirable consequences such as withdrawal of funding. In this technology policy initiative, the Victorian education department has produced a corporate template which makes everything seem possible, although there will inevitably be great variability in the extent to which the different elements are taken up.

IMPLICATIONS FOR THE POLICY ROLES OF TEACHERS

These are, of course, the merest sketches of a small sample of policies relevant to the interface between literacy, technology and learning. Our aim is not to provide comprehensive coverage—rather, to illustrate from typical cases the kinds of tasks and challenges that face teachers in their various policy roles, and to underline the need for schools to take policy work seriously at the school level. The things we have to say on the basis of our survey of these policies will hold to a large extent for the other Australian states as well as for international policy scenes.

It is clear that schools and teachers face a daunting task when it comes to interpreting and prioritising policies, translating them into coherent plans and programs, and implementing the policies in the classroom. For a start, there are some significant tensions—at times, downright contradictions—between policies at different levels and across different curriculum areas. How are schools, for example, to handle the requirements of the national literacy plan with its emphasis on 'foundational [print-centred] literacy' in conjunction with acknowledging the arrival of the I-generation: students who 'interact effortlessly with the new information and communications media'? How do we reconcile 'back-to-basics' emphases—with their premium on teacher/expert-driven diagnosis, intervention, and drill-and-skill packages for elementary competency development—with the challenge to build a learning environment that looks beyond 'foundational' literacy from the earliest opportunity? Moreover, how do we build a learning environment that 'look[s] beyond "computer literacy" and consider[s] the importance of "information literacy" which takes into account the development of higher-order skills in processing information' (Tinkler et al. 1996: x)?

At a much more specific level, what does it mean to act on the principle of incorporating computers into effective learning in ways that ensure equitable access, participation, and effective outcomes for students? How is this policy requirement to be interpreted? Is it equitable access within the classroom walls, or do we take into account individual students' out-of-school access, to sources of expertise as well as to equipment? In a policy-driven era, where schools have devolved onto teachers responsibility and account-ability for actualising policy 'desiderata' (expressed in a few easy words, but behind which may lurk huge logistical challenges at the level of implementation), just how are teachers to interpret and translate into practical action and material outcomes something as seemingly innocent as 'ensuring equitable outcomes for students'?

Which policy texts should we pay most heed to, and how do we decide how much heed to pay to different and competing values and recommendations? *Converging Technology, Work and Learning* (NBEET 1995) charges education with the responsibility of equipping the community and workforce with the skills necessary for exploiting new technologies. This resonates with the idea of efficacious learning, connecting what learners do here and now with what they do elsewhere and later (Gee, Hull & Lankshear 1996). But if we accept this do we, for example, go along with the kind of competency-based accounts of 'skills' that prevail in NBEET documents, or do we aim for a more thoroughgoing 'sociocultural' view of effective practice, which insists on taking account of operational, cultural and critical dimensions? What are teachers to do where departmental policies seem at one point (for example, in a computer guidelines policy) to settle for performance of 'skills', but seem elsewhere to insist that learners 'make meaning out of experience' (for example, in a policy on effective learning and teaching principles)? After all, when push comes to shove, it is performance against 'benchmarks' that matters as far as accountability is concerned. And it is far from clear whether 'meaning-making', in the strong sense integral to a sociocultural approach to literacy, has much to do with 'benchmarking'.

A similar issue arises in policies that speak of 'learning technologies' as a powerful tool for helping students achieve important learning outcomes. If this translates most obviously into an emphasis on the operational dimension of subject literacies and curriculum practices, how do we promote a more sophisticated understanding of 'technology' among our colleagues to achieve learning in the other dimensions as well?

Then there are those 'gaps' in policy texts that seem to arise at the precise points where we most need guidance and substance. In the *Digital Rhetorics* project we looked in vain for strong examples of curriculum policy development that showed signs of serious cross-curriculum consultation and collaboration. We looked for evidence that ideas about what is involved in promoting technological literacy in the English KLA had been developed in conversation with developing ideas of what counts as technological literacy in the Studies of Society and Environment KLAs or in Science. Where can we turn for assistance in our efforts to develop coherent and effective programs for technological literacy across the curriculum— that will carry over into community and work-based practices—if 'literacy' is spoken about only in the English KLA, and then in predominantly literary and 'print-centric' terms? Specifically, how might we aim in our programs for 'effective coverage' of a skills and concepts base in the area of new communication and information technologies, in ways that make best use of our available human and material resources and avoid unnecessary duplication, but that promote productive overlap and practice between KLAs?

We could continue to raise such questions, but schools and teachers seek solutions and strategies as well as legitimate questions; they appreciate being offered some clues as well as tasks, snags and challenges. This book intends to be in the business of tackling both ends of these equations. Four points apply here.

First, we need to be clear that teachers' work nowadays is very much policy-directed, and that teachers more than previously have to become policy readers, policy critics, policy interpreters, and principled policy implementers. We cannot just lump this in with the 'admin' part of the job. Handling 'assessing and reporting' is enhanced where these practices are continuous extensions of coherent programs based on school-level policies; which translate official curriculum requirements into manageable tasks; for which staff have been 'suitably professionally developed'; where the school has developed a coherent 'ethos' and 'culture'; such that the work of each teacher is augmented by the work of others, who share a common understanding of how we 'make these confounded policies work'. Policy work is not an optional extra for the effective teacher: it is now fundamental to success in the job, whether we like it or not.

Second, as we argue in chapter 6, this 'policy work' at the school level is not a job to be done by one or two 'leaders' or by heads of departments. It is best done across staff as a whole. The phenomena of 'gaps', fragmentation and compartmentalisation, tensions and contradictions across different 'bits', the partiality and 'ad-hocery' of so much policy activity at national and state levels, are instructive here. If we want to get coherence, efficiency and synergy into our policy implementation, we need to model these virtues in our policy work at school level. This means doing it as teams and as 'wholes', not as individuals or separate interest groups. It means doing it across subject areas, in collaboration. It means tackling policy development in conjunction with school-based and coordinated professional development. (Practical suggestions emerging from this kind of holistic approach are presented in chapter 6.)

Third, to take account of our policy roles intelligently and successfully is not a matter of simply reading policy texts. As we have suggested, understanding the policy context calls for sound understanding of the wider—all the way to the global-level—contexts within which national, state, and local policy deliberations take place. If we think we can deal with policies tackling the interface between literacy, technology and learning without a working understanding of 'the information society', 'the new work order', and 'communities of practice associated with new communication and information technologies', we are probably gravely mistaken. Likewise, we
to recognise the extent to which appropriate portions of resear
theoretical literatures are relevant to understanding, inter

critiquing and implementing policies. To understand the national literacy plan for what it is and what it is not, we need to read and understand texts like Shirley Brice Heath's (1983) *Ways with Words*, and James Gee's (1996) *Social Linguistics and Literacies*, among many others, taking in *Australia's Literacies* (Lo Bianco & Freebody 1997) along the way. (We would like to add that this book is intended to help with a lot of these 'extra tasks'. The following chapters describe, examine and analyse classroom work being done at the interface between literacy, technology and learning, to suggest how pedagogical practices in this area can be enhanced. We refer to ideas, based on theory and research, advanced in chapter 2, and to descriptions of 'patterns' and 'principles' evident in school-based teaching and learning that provide clues for how to progress in the literacy–technology project, presented in chapter 5.)

Fourth, at best, policy can be an effective guide for teachers—to be interpreted, translated and implemented. The strategy for teachers is to approach the policy critically, compare it with something that they know works, recognise the elements that are not desirable, then adapt and manipulate it to make it suit their particular context. At a time when there is a flurry of activity in the policy area to put new technologies on the school agenda, teachers need to ensure that their curriculum priorities are firmly established, that there is clear articulation between different curriculum areas in policy practice, that literacy and technology people talk to each other in the process of policy formation, and that decisions are informed by a sociocultural understanding of literacy and technology practice. Literacy teachers can refuse or, at very least, question whatever aspects of policy implementation they find unacceptable, and look for ways to subvert it in practice. They can also engage in critically informed and purposeful policy-formation work. Striving to build support for a socioculturally informed 3D view of literacy is an important option here. But it also means organising and working through professional associations, and through school-level programming and planning committees, in support of educationally expansive rather than narrowly constrained constructions of literacy, technology and learning.

An example of effective literacy, technology and learning policy formation

The earlier portraits of Caldwell, New Park and Ealing provided useful insight into the different ways schools may approach policy formation at the local level. Caldwell did not have a formal literacy, technology and learning policy, the principal preferring to deal with issues as they appeared. At New Park, although there was a quite well-developed, ambitious, written policy in place, only two members of staff had any interest in exploring the technologies' potential for learning and teaching, which made their impact minimal. By contrast, Ealing Grammar had a carefully conceived, elaborate whole-school policy, although this was implemented in the absence of formal policy documentation.

We conclude this chapter by sketching another school's forays into policy formation to see what else we might learn from a particular approach at the school level. Classroom practice at Abbotsdale is presented in chapter 4. Here we describe its broad strategy for developing policy at the literacy–technology–learning interface—a strategy in which the Year 5 teacher, Robert, played a leading role.

Abbotsdale

Abbotsdale has well-developed technology and language policies. The technology policy follows the national *Statement on Technology for Australian Schools* (Curriculum Corporation 1994c) in distinguishing between technology as 'a learning area' and technology as 'learning technology', referring to computer uses in classrooms. It also observes the four strands in the national statement: designing, making and appraising; materials; information; and systems. Technology is not taught as a discrete subject in primary schools in the state, and so Abbotsdale's policy is to undertake designing, making and appraising activities in relation to materials, information and systems within other subject areas—for example, specifying, gathering, sorting and analysing information needed in classroom activities (heights, news, distances, opinions, issues), and recognising the impact of information on learners' lives. The learning aim is to alert students to technology as a way of thinking, acting, proceeding—a form of practice—engaged in by humans at all times, in all places, within the various spheres of their daily lives. Students should learn to think and act in 'technological' ways, just as they learn to think and act from aesthetic, moral, economic, scientific and other points of view. The school aims to provide a balance of activities across the four technology 'strands'.

With a teacher-librarian from a neighbouring school and

the region's learning technology project officer, Robert has framed a careful sequence of skills and conceptual leanings designed to make optimal use of the school's learning technology resources (see chapter 6 for further details). Concepts and skills are related within the learning sequence. Opening files, changing fonts, manipulating graphics and the like are simultaneously skills and concepts. As such, they are to be acquired as far as possible within appropriate—natural and functional—contexts (Gee 1996).

Abbotsdale's language policy, expressed in its English program statement, is based closely on the state's *English Syllabus for Years 1 to 10* (Department of Education, Queensland 1994b), which makes only occasional and brief explicit references to the nature and the role of new technologies. These references, however, are within the context of the social practices and discourses of contemporary life, to which subject English must respond and be accountable.

The syllabus is strongly dominated by literary and grammar overtones that emphasise conventional print texts and 'media texts' (film, print and TV advertisements) over digitally coded texts. Its underlying ideas are, however, in principle conducive to developing a meta-level awareness of language: for example, learners are to 'know' genres—to become proficient with the genres integral to effective participation in everyday life. Teachers are exhorted to make the purposes, generic structures, linguistic features and cultural contexts of text production and functions explicit.

Drawing closely on the state English syllabus, learning at Abbotsdale is based on a text-context model of language, according to which meaning is realised through purposefully constructed texts generated within functional contexts. Texts are conceived as spoken, written, non-verbal, visual or auditory in type. The relationship between text and context is understood in terms of cultural context and social context. All language is seen to arise within activities called genres which are engaged at the level of cultural context. At the same time, variables emerging in the social context influence language use at the level of register. Variations occur around four aspects: 'field' (which has to do with the subject matter); 'tenor' (which involves roles and relationships); 'medium' (written, spoken, visual); and 'mode' (for example, film, telephone, newspaper).

Against this background, Abbotsdale identifies its language

learning in terms of 'functional' and 'operational' aims. Its functional aim is to help students learn to use language effectively to participate as confident members of family and community, engage in further study, and take part in a range of recreational pursuits. Its operational aim is to develop students' abilities to produce and understand written and spoken English fluently, effectively, appropriately and critically for a wide range of personal and social purposes.

The policy claims language is best developed through modelling and scaffolding, recognising individual learning styles and rates of learning, offering meaningful experiences across a range of genres, promoting positive attitudes towards language use, through explicit celebration of students' language skills; valuing and building on prior experiences and attainments; and valuing culture, gender, class, physical and intellectual diversity.

Three types of learning activity are to be planned in accordance with the learning styles of the students, within three identifiable phases of language development. All types of activity and all phases of development should be taken into account and planned to maximise independent control of language skills and understandings. The types of activity are called 'real-life', 'lifelike', and 'focused' learning episodes. Real-life activities involve exposure to genres and their embedded language uses in situ. Lifelike activities are classroom approximations to the 'real thing'. Focused learning episodes involve detailed practice in specific elements of language use, such as drafting and redrafting a particular kind of text until it is produced 'properly'.

The three phases seen as leading to independent control are an 'incidental' learning phase, an 'explicit' learning phase, and an 'extended' learning phase. Incidental learning usually involves prior exposure to a genre and its associated text types outside the formal planned teaching and learning setting. Classroom learning, in other words, should build on prior outside experience as far as possible. The explicit learning phase involves introductory and planned exposure to the object of learning. Extended learning will occur within and outside the planned learning setting. The teacher's role here is to help maintain the language, provide continued support and present opportunities for extended focus on skills and understandings.

The school's technology policy is coherent, comprehensive and integrated with other policies—notably its language policy. For Robert's Year 5 classroom, as we see in chapter 4, the concept of developing programming closely in relation to planning works well and, assuming roughly equal competence across the staff, would work well at the whole-school level. Part of what makes it work at Abbotsdale is that each teacher has a circumscribed range of operational competencies to develop among students, and these are arranged in a logical sequence. This makes it possible to give focused attention to the cultural and critical dimensions of using new technologies within literacy practices, as the teacher is freed from having to teach any- or everything at the operational level alone.

We return to the question of how schools might approach effective policy formation to meet their local needs in chapter 6. In chapter 4 we look at some more classrooms to extend our understanding of the ways in which teachers and students have been grappling with the challenges of integrating literacy, technology and learning.

# 4

Classroom portraits: learning from everyday practices

BACK TO THE SITES

In chapter 1 we presented portraits of classroom practices in three contrasting sites. Our aim was to capture some of the ways in which teachers and administrators are responding to the technology–literacy challenge. We found a great deal of energy, enthusiasm and initiative, on the part of teachers and learners alike, for integrating new technologies into the activities of classroom-based literacy education. At the same time, as we noted in those initial portraits, we found features that affect the quality of classroom teaching and learning in ways we need to think about carefully. In particular, we found evidence of:

- uneven development between different sites;
- various forms of discontinuity and vulnerability;
- doubts, suspicions and even fears on the part of some teachers and parents;
- tensions between competing values, goals, understandings and priorities within sites, which sometimes generated resistance;
- the adoption of different strategies from school to school for tackling development and change in the area of literacy and new technologies;
- a 'business-as-usual' syndrome, whereby literacy activities

involving new technologies tended to look similar to familiar practices built around previous technologies.

Of course, the portraits presented in chapter 1 involved just three of twenty classrooms across eleven sites investigated in the larger study on which this book is based. There was considerable overlap across all the sites, such that the features identified in chapter 1 were apparent to a large extent in other places as well. Even so, we observed further important features, trends, and patterns that we need to acknowledge and explore.

Here we look at five additional sites, involving six schools and eight classrooms. They range from lower-primary to upper-secondary levels and cover urban as well as rural settings. Together with the sites described in chapter 1, they pretty well cover the range of what we found in the study as a whole. For each of the following portraits we describe the site, participants, resources, teaching and learning aims, and key features of the classrooms and practices observed. On this basis, we identify some of the significant issues for classroom-based literacy education involving new technologies raised by each portrait.

The issues associated with classroom practice that emerge in this chapter must be considered in conjunction with the features described in chapter 1, along with the theoretical considerations tackled in chapter 2 and the main points emerging from our discussion of policy in chapter 3. They are all part of the larger 'reality' we are trying to understand and respond to. This chapter completes our description of those examples from the general scene of literacy–technology education in Australia investigated in the original study.

THE FIVE PORTRAITS

1 Abbotsdale: informed practice in a Year 5 classroom

Abbotsdale is a P–7 school with 230 students who are mainly white Australian working-class young people from semi-urban and rural homes, including caravan parks. It is located in a regional rural service centre some 200 kilometres from the state capital. The school has for several years been officially designated a 'disadvantaged school'.

The Year 5 class comprises 24 students—11 girls and 13 boys—overwhelmingly from low-income (including unemployed or underemployed) and, occasionally, low–middle-income homes. All are native English speakers. Robert, the teacher, has 22 years' teaching experience, the last ten of them at Abbotsdale. He is an active teacher-researcher, familiar with constructivist approaches to learning, with theories about development of self and beliefs about self, and with principles and practices of inclusive learning—all of which he integrates with his understandings of theory and research related to the use of computer applications in learning.

Robert is comfortable with new technologies. Having been around computers for fifteen years, he recounts how they were demystified for him when a friend demonstrated a fully functional unit which had the motherboard attached to a piece of timber. He upgrades the computers in his classroom himself, troubleshoots other teachers' computer hassles and oversees software acquisitions. He is studying part-time for his PhD, investigating the role of teachers and technologies in promoting the development of higher-order thinking skills in children with intellectual disabilities.

From time to time a Year 7 student, Amanda, attends the class, invited by Robert to act as a peer tutor when new computing skills are being introduced. When she arrived at Abbotsdale in Year 2—at which time she had virtually no reading or writing skills and lacked social and communication capabilities—Amanda was clinically assessed as 'moderately intellectually disabled'. By Year 5 she was still withdrawn socially, and assiduously avoided anything to do with reading and writing, other than copying sentences from books straight into her notepad. She was, however, fascinated by computers. Robert built on this interest and designed an individualised program for Amanda, aimed at enabling her to develop a repertoire of language and literacy processes, understandings and competencies while she worked on desktop publication and drawing applications—gradually moving her toward text production. In a short period her reading and writing abilities soared. Moreover, Amanda was soon recognised by her classmates as an expert in desktop publishing, and they sought her help regularly. Robert coached her in a number of peer-tutoring strategies and she ran 'workshops' for students during class time. Over a period of three years, her communication skills and self-confidence improved dramatically.

The classroom is equipped with three upgraded computers

with 486 and 586 equivalent processing speeds. Two are fitted with CD-ROM drives; the other is linked to the internet via a local public provider. Other resources include a hand-held scanner, a colour-enabled Desk Jet printer, several CD-ROMs, movie-making software, MS Publisher, and problem-solving software. There is also a class set of resource books on inventions and inventors, and a range of printed 'scaffolds' developed by Robert for use in class activities. These include worksheets, task sheets, checklists, and guidelines for activities.

At present the class is undertaking an integrated cross-curriculum, theme-based unit of work on 'inventions'. Learners are to produce film narratives (movie scripts), biographies, reports, poster advertisements, invitations, explanations, justifications, evaluations and procedural accounts, as constitutive elements of the overall unit. These outcomes all accord with the state's English syllabus, which is strongly based in genre theory. Centrepieces of the unit include a short, animated movie (using Microsoft 3D MovieMaker) on an invention, and an oral presentation of a written report on the social impact of selected inventions. These outcome goals provide the 'glue' for the diverse genres the students engage with, as they produce posters to advertise their movie, invitations to the premiere using computer software, and wrestle with the pros and cons of specific inventions from the standpoint of different social groups and environments affected by them. While learning tasks and experiences in this unit are at best reasonable approximations to 'real-life' social practices, the pedagogy is rich in 'lifelike' practices and 'focused learning episodes'.

In his strategy for embedding new technologies in classroom language and literacy education, via a theme-based approach to cross-curriculum planning, Robert carefully incorporates lifelike learning opportunities and resources into classroom literacy events. For example, lifelike learning experiences are engaged when students using desktop publishing software are required to design and produce a poster advertising their movie, and invitations to the movie's premiere, in addition to constructing scripts for their group's movie, made using Microsoft's 3D MovieMaker. However, it is not a 'real-life' activity, in that the students do not prepare their movies for an audience beyond the class or even screen their movies for a whole-class audience.

Robert uses the pedagogical device of activity rotations to handle themes like 'inventions' as cross-curriculum units of work.

Large chunks of time—90-minute blocks both sides of a break, each block divided into three 30-minute segments—are set aside every week. During these segments, small groups of three to six students, who remain together for the duration of the work unit, move through cycles of activities and tasks in different spatial locations. Within each sequence, the 30-minute segments are devoted to different kinds of activities, which usually draw on different communications and information technologies. One involves reading print-based materials related to the theme (sometimes aloud to a teacher aide). This is for reading practice as well as for getting information relevant to the projects. The second segment involves working in groups with pen, paper, worksheets, preset tasks, and discussion. This segment is concerned with preparing ideas and components to be implemented at the computers. The third segment involves work at the computers.

During rotations, Robert's plan is that each group moves through two complete sequences of activities to maintain a rate of focused progress, to ensure continuity, and to provide for integration of reading, writing, discussing and computing activities. Following rotation sequences, the class typically comes together· to discuss issues, problems and discoveries. The unit of work as a whole comprises a complex array of integrated, interlocking and interrelated text-based activities. These inform and build on each other, culminating in the production of reports that draw on the total range of texts produced.

The teaching and learning practices are marked by an emphasis on learning through technologies while learning about technologies. Pedagogy is strongly and consciously informed by theory. A mix of conventional and innovative approaches to teaching and learning is employed to integrate the use of technology into activities. Classroom activities are scaffolded in various ways. They include using oral and written questions, which prompt students to reflect individually or in groups on a process or tool and to evaluate it (for example, a piece of software or a reference book), and using task and guide sheets, which assist students to work from cognitively simple knowledge to more complex understandings (for example, through questions requiring students to evaluate, extrapolate, analyse and synthesise content and processes). These activities enact Robert's constructivist theories of learning and present opportunities to experiment, explore, play, take risks and solve problems using conventional resources as well as new technologies. Robert actively cultivates a culture of inquiry, exploration and self-evaluation which encourages students to be self-motivated and successful learners. At the same time, students are modelling skills for others, providing answers to questions, and suggesting explanations for events and processes.

Robert's deliberate focus is always on developing students' meta-level understandings of problem-solving processes and strategies, which is precisely what the state's P–10 English syllabus calls for. The syllabus also advocates development of a classroom culture that enlists teachers and students as members of 'a community of learners', sharing contexts and purposes for learning. For Robert, computer technologies provide new contexts in which to learn. He insists that the technologies do not become ends in themselves. Instead, they are employed in ways designed to maximise learning in general, and the development and practices of higher-order thinking skills in particular.

In Robert's classroom the roles of teacher, learner and collaborator are never static or fixed. At times, Robert teaches a particular concept. At other times, concepts and processes become reference points, particularly when introducing new software. Students use each other as learning resources, exemplified in Amanda tutoring the Year 5 students and in the ways learners turn to each other for assistance, advice and feedback during small-group and whole-class sessions. They turn to Robert only when a problem or question proves too much for their own resources. Similarly, guided participation is an organic component of the teaching-learning process in his class. Networks of interaction with students working in pairs and small groups, discussing, arguing, negotiating and evaluating, are all especially evident in computer-mediated text production.

Abbotsdale illustrates five key issues, each of which has implications for classroom-based learning. These are: the relationship between theory and practice; the potential for fragility within the site; planning and programming links; the relationship between classroom purposes and technology purchases; and possibilities for operating as a community of learners in school settings. We now discuss each briefly.

First, Abbotsdale highlights the value of teachers informing their practice with mature and cogent theory. Robert can draw on the full range of approaches to language and literacy education that have been adopted in the state during the past 20 years, and integrate them into coherent practice. He is a teacher-researcher and a researcher-teacher, currently doing his PhD and subjecting his own classroom pedagogy to rigorous, theorised scrutiny. At a time when teachers in the state are faced with a complicated, hybridised English syllabus, much of which is informed by complex theory, saddled with ever-escalating assessment and reporting demands, and where the profession is beleaguered by widespread charges of failing to perform its role adequately, Robert never appears pressured in his work. His technological expertise at the operational level is augmented by his theoretical perspective on learning, as well as his understanding of social applications of new technologies. The clear implication here is that preparing teachers within preservice and in-service initiatives to integrate new technologies effectively into classroom pedagogy involves more than merely 'skilling them up'. What is needed are extended opportunities to make explicit and concrete connections between theory and practice.

Second, the Abbotsdale study illustrates the benefit of teachers having grounded experience with computer technologies, especially to accomplish specific curricular goals in the context of a classroom with limited computer resources. Robert has been around computers for a long time and understands their 'logic'. On the other hand, his personal expertise and status as a key player in the technology side of life at Abbotsdale raises the issue of 'fragility'. What would happen if suddenly he were to leave? Would the machines continue to be maintained? Would other teachers have access to onsite competence when the machines went down? To whom could other teachers turn for advice? The issue of fragility underscores the importance of whole-school approaches to developing competence.

The third issue concerns the relationship between planning and programming. Abbotsdale students benefit from the school's technology policy being coherent, comprehensive and integrated with the language and literacy policy. Positioned as he is in relation to computer-based technologies, Robert is able to enhance his language and literacy teaching with informed technological expertise, just as he can enhance his technology-related teaching by coupling it to a sound approach to building language across the curriculum. The development of programming closely in relation to planning works well. Each teacher at Abbotsdale has a circumscribed range of operational competencies to promote among students, and these are arranged in a logical sequence. This makes it possible to give focused attention to the cultural and critical dimensions of using new technologies within literacy practices. The implication here is that in-school planning and policy development within language, literacy and technology should occur at the whole-school level and in an integrated way.

The fourth issue concerns the relationship between classroom purposes and technology purchases. There is no wasteful or duplicating purchase of hardware and software apparent at Abbotsdale. Tailoring scope and sequence within the technology policy and planning scope and sequence within the English program (and vice versa) enables the development of overt literacy education purposes in Robert's curriculum. The implication is that the clearer and more systematic a school can become about its related language and technology purposes, the easier it is to make intelligent and cost-effective resourcing decisions.

The final issue points to possibilities for and advantages of operating as a community of learners within school settings. Developing a community of learners in the Abbotsdale classroom has implications for the quality of learning and the realisation of important educational values, which are often espoused but less often apparent: for example, enhancing self-esteem, increasing motivation, and practising collaboration and cooperation.

2 Tipping and Danton: facing the technology literacy challenge in a remote rural area

This portrait covers two remote rural schools—one primary, the other secondary—in the same administrative area. Along with many other schools, spread over thousands of square kilometres, Tipping and Danton are served by a single learning technology education adviser, Georgia. Our account focuses on how participants face the challenges of limited local knowledge and equipment, unreliable internet access and restricted time with Georgia, who covers vast distances by road and on whose great energy and commitment each school relies heavily.

Tipping and Danton share four significant features: multi-age classes to accommodate the small student populations; Georgia, who provides technology support for the region; curriculum guidelines produced by the state English syllabus, the departmental 'computers in use' policy and the state funding allocations for provision of computers in schools; and Commonwealth funding, used to increase technological resources for schools in isolated, rural and low socioeconomic communities.

Tipping Primary is a P–7 school serving a remote grain-production area, 500 kilometres from the state capital. The population is almost entirely white Australian. The school has 53 male and female students, 18 of whom are in Teresa's composite Year 5–7 class. They are housed in a spacious classroom. Teresa has been teaching at Tipping for ten years and majored in Computer Studies during her preservice teacher education. The other key participant in this site is, of course, Georgia. Her work involves providing technical advice about school technology resources, running lessons for teachers and students in hardware and software applications, conducting in-service professional development sessions for teachers at the regional support centre, and arranging and coordinating exchanges of equipment and advice among schools in her area. In addition, she works with the teachers to envisage and plan computer-mediated learning activities, and participates in these wherever appropriate and possible. Georgia's preferred pedagogical mode is to work with teachers to develop motivated, coherent activities around applications she is trialling. When we visited Tipping, she was exploring potential learning applications of a digital camera and scanner, in conjunction with the use of the internet and HyperCard. Georgia works with the teachers under her care to conceptualise learning activities and projects, trains them and the students in relevant applications, and coordinates with all schools in her area to visit on a schedule that keeps the various activities moving forward as efficiently as possible.

Teresa's class has access to two Apple IIe computers with Image Writer printers, one Macintosh LC639, and a Macintosh LC45 equipped with a modem, an external CD-ROM drive, an HP Deskwriter 600 printer, plus a dedicated phone line, and microphone. Internet applications are sometimes used in conjunction with a Conferlink telephone for French lessons with a specialist teacher located in a distant town. The class also has occasional access to a scanner, digital camera, CD-ROM burner, and a Macintosh LD630, courtesy of Georgia. Apart from internet applications, the main software used includes HyperCard, ClarisWorks, and a variety of drill-and-skill games (for example, Mathsblaster).

Tipping is in the process of updating and rewriting its computer policy to reflect the state's official guidelines for the use of computers in learning. Policies and circumstances governing the quality and quantity of resources available strongly influence classroom practice at Tipping. The state education department began an organised approach to computer allocation and purchase some years previously through its Year 6/7 computer policy, which allocated computers according to the number of students in Year 7 and then the number in Year 6. Provision for upgrading resources, however, was not made through this program. Furthermore, the Internet Service Provider (ISP) used at Tipping is expensive and unreliable—a function of telecommunications underdevelopment in remote areas. Phone equipment and lines are outmoded. When computer hardware fails and needs repair it must go 500 kilometres for servicing. Technical advice for glitches that could be fixed on site involves phone calls to the regional school support centre, hundreds of kilometres away. The fragility and vulnerability of equipment inclines Teresa to prohibit unsupervised student use, and doors are kept locked when necessary. A recent hard-drive 'crash' put the best computer out of action for an entire school term.

Teaching and learning objectives for language and literacy activities include developing an understanding of biography as a distinctive genre, undertaking a cross-curriculum unit of work on 'The Universe', with an emphasis on understanding and employing orientating, enhancing and synthesising activities (as specified in the English syllabus) and, for Years 6 and 7 students, learning aspects of French language and culture by way of the internet. The teacher sees the students acquiring 'old skills, but applying them in a new way' (via new technologies): for example, decoding and encoding fluently; using literacy skills and understandings involved in researching and reporting biographical information; reading and deciding what is relevant; note-taking, scanning and collecting information selectively.

Three main activities are in evidence. In the first, students work from information presented by the teacher to compile and represent biographical information about national sportspersons according to a generic structure of name, date of birth, event, background. These are assembled as HyperCard presentations from which the education adviser subsequently burns a CD-ROM that she gives to the class. In the second activity, use of the internet and CD-ROMs replaces HyperCard as the new technology focus. Besides searching CD-ROMs, books, and magazines, students use email and the World Wide Web to pursue information about 'Space', and produce work in accordance with the orientating, enhancing and synthesising sequence. Here, as in the biographies project, texts are roughed out and drafted using pen and paper. In the third regular ongoing activity, Year 6 and Year 7 students engage twice weekly in French lessons with students from other isolated schools and the 'remote' French teacher.

More significant than the outcomes in this site are impediments to what the students could achieve occasioned by aspects of the technologies. During the 'Universe' project, the internet connection failed each time the students tried to use it. On one occasion, Teresa located and bookmarked sites on 'Planets' after school was finished for the day, and timetabled the class next morning to go to the computer six at a time. However, she could not get a connection. Most of the small-group lessons planned to teach students specialised skills in the new technologies are interrupted by technical hitches—problems Teresa does not feel confident to deal with. She volunteers that these interruptions 'distort the students' understandings of the process'. Not surprisingly, students we interviewed cannot explain the structure of the HyperCard presentation, the technical skills required to construct a presentation, nor how to use the camera or scanner.

The same and worse occurs in the French lessons. The Electronic Classroom was established by the department to enable students in Years 6 and 7 to take part in the mandatory LOTE program. Equipment given to schools included the Macintosh LC475, modem, phone line, microphones and the Conferlink phone housed in the tiny room off Teresa's classroom. Twice a week, Year 6 and Year 7 students engage in French lessons with students from four other isolated schools and a French teacher based in a large town in the region. The students are supposed to sit in front of the computer and download from the machine graphics fed in by the teacher who is talking to them on the telephone. Difficulties encountered include: poor telephone connections, causing phone calls to be cut off; the small 4 Meg RAM on the computer, leading to computer 'freezing'; an incongruence between visual and audio reception, resulting in instructions from the teacher being irrelevant or insufficient; poor visual reception, responsible for students missing important sections of the lesson; and poor audio connection, where students often cannot hear other students or the teacher. Support for the Electronic Classroom is minimal. Any failed equipment is sent away, advice is obtained via lengthy, expensive STD phone calls, and a request for an upgrade of the computer's RAM size was refused.

Like Tipping, Danton is a tiny settlement, 90 kilometres from the nearest large town, with a hotel, the school, a motel, general store, service station, newsagent, stock agent, and some other small businesses that take advantage of passing tourist traffic. The school is a combined primary and secondary school, with 100 students in the P–7 primary section, and 20 in the Years 8–10 secondary department. The students are again mainly white Australian, many of whom come in from stations to attend.

The group of students at the centre of our study are Year 8–10 Business Studies students who are working with the teacher on a project during lessons, lunchtimes, and in study breaks. They are not really a class at all but a group gathered together for an extracurricular 'learning opportunity project' as the end of year breakup draws near. Their teacher, Denise, has only recently returned to full-time teaching after some years at home caring for children. As a Business Studies teacher, Denise feels the impact of new technologies keenly. When she began teaching, manual typewriters were used to train mainly girls in typing skills. On her return, Denise finds that computers have largely displaced electric typewriters, and the typing skills component of the Business Studies syllabus has been replaced with key-boarding skills. She is acutely aware of Danton's geographic and social isolation from 'mainstream Australia'. She often expresses concern that the community may be cut off from ideas, and that important changes and opportunities in the cities are passing them by. Denise is committed to doing all she can to ensure that Danton's students get every opportunity to experience 'current technologies'. The remaining participant in this study is Georgia.

As already mentioned, the young participants are not really a class at all but a group of a dozen volunteer students working on a HyperCard presentation to be used during their end-of-year speech night. The project is an example of a fine act of pedagogical opportunism on Denise's part. Like Tipping, Danton receives Commonwealth funding for socioeconomically and geographically disadvantaged schools, and has used the funding to increase its computing resources. This funding, however, requires making submissions adhering to Commonwealth government priorities. At the time of our visit, Danton had just heard that its submission for extra technological equipment had been rejected. Danton has access to four Macintosh Performas, three Mac Classics, a Pentium PC won by a student in an art competition, an Apple printer, and software including Claris-Works and HyperCard. Georgia's availability means the school can also get access to a QuickTake camera, a scanner, a more powerful Macintosh 630CD, and cables that connect it to a VCR. Denise attempts to maximise access to this equipment, motivated by her commitment to grasp every possible opportunity for her students to experience and learn how to use 'current technology'.

Knowing that it would soon be time for the principal's end-of-year speech, Denise was quick to take advantage of the occasion as a pretext for organising the group of students around a project, and to make use of Georgia's expertise and of equipment not available at school. Seeing presentation software (like HyperCard stacks) as 'stuff of the urban present'—a common tool in business circles, and increasingly popular in school settings—she throws herself into organising, teaching and learning with these students, with Georgia's input, to create an effective HyperCard presentation for a specific purpose within the larger life of the school.

The aim of this extracurricular activity is to produce a specific outcome—a suitable HyperCard presentation to accompany the principal's speech—and, in the process, for students to learn how to drive the equipment involved. The presentation is designed to be integrated into the speech by presenting images of the school year. These images are produced with the QuickTake camera, video frames from film shot by students, and photographs scanned into the computer. The production process is broken into specific tasks, delegated to individuals or pairs of students who have 'contracted' with Denise to complete these tasks. At times, Denise meets the 'team' as a group, and in between they report to her with their artefacts. As speech day approaches, a sense of urgency surrounds the completion of tasks.

Work must coincide with Georgia's visits to the school. It spills into class time, lunchtimes, any available moment. Student assessment activities are also in full cry. Some students are observed taking typing tests. During class time, the Business

Studies Centre is filled with students completing diverse tasks, curricular and otherwise: typing tests, downloading images from the QuickTake camera, building links to slides in HyperCard, completing word-processing assignments for Year 8 English, producing invitations for speech night, completing balance sheets for Business Principles, selecting photographs to be scanned by Georgia. Lunch breaks are signalled by some students arriving, some departing, and others keeping on task. Denise stays for the lunch break, and directs students in their activities.

When Georgia is there, Denise and the students often gather to learn skills. If Georgia is working with students downloading images from the QuickTake camera to the computer, or something similar, Denise is hovering nearby, asking questions and taking part in the 'lesson'. Sometimes Georgia serves as technician rather than teacher. We see her scanning images from conventional cameras into the computer, on her own and at lunchtime.

As end-of-year distractions compete with project tasks, initial student enthusiasm begins to wane. Denise starts a lunchtime session, reminding students: 'We're all in this together, otherwise it won't work'. Time and equipment constraints are pressing. They have only two days to access the scanner, the computer and Georgia. Denise recaps the previous meeting, prompting students for the configuration of stacks she suggested last week: three stacks of unlimited 'cards' or slides built around the outline the principal has written for her speech. Denise recommends using just three different backgrounds for the presentation—one for each stack—and allocates the job of taking a digital shot of the school garden and administration block for the first stack to one of the boys.

Denise discusses the notion of audience for the presentation—parents and visitors—emphasising that the students are actually working for the principal in preparing the presentation. Pairs and subgroups have been given specific tasks, such as using the digital camera to photograph tuckshop staff and specialist teachers (including physical education and music teachers), grabbing image stills from video and converting them to digital images, interviewing staff and students, or using text-art software to create headings and the like. Denise spends the rest of lunchtime checking progress and working with two students charged with setting up the 'cards' on the computer. With time short, she merely demonstrates to the students how to use the equipment, and explains as economically as possible the steps needed to complete their respective tasks. At the end, much of the fine-tuning, the pulling together and the final construction falls to Georgia and Denise, but enough of the assigned tasks have been completed to ensure delivery on time. We find out subsequently that the presentation was a great success.

Tipping and Danton suggest four further important issues for classroom-based learning at the interface of literacy, learning and new technologies.

First, it is useful to consider what is sometimes called the 'old wine in new bottles' syndrome (Lankshear & Bigum, in press), which resonates with what we referred to as 'business as usual' in the chapter 1 portraits. This is the idea that people will be 'using old skills but applying them in new ways' when they engage in future practices involving literacy and technologies. In many cases, we find the skills used in research for HyperCard and PowerPoint presentations essentially 'the same, and set up in the same ways' as those formerly employed in pen-and-paper contexts. And the activities themselves are often familiar to anyone acquainted with elementary school classrooms. To a large extent, the substance of the learning and teaching remains more or less the same as we knew it to be prior to the emergence of these new technologies. It has merely been 'technologised' under a new technology regime. This response is not, of course, unexpected. Teachers have been presented with new technologies and been expected to make them work. In the absence of good curriculum and pedagogical leadership from those directing the changes, or from people charged in advance with working out how schools can use new technologies in learning most effectively, teachers have little option other than to fall back on what they already know. The challenge here is by no means one for teachers alone: it cuts across policy, administrative, research, teacher education and planning domains.

Second, much more than in the earlier portraits we get a powerful sense here of teachers facing the literacy–technology challenge under extraordinarily difficult conditions. In part, these difficulties were matters of availability of physical resources and technological support. But they were also matters of knowledge, understanding and experience of integrating new technologies into pedagogy in appropriate ways. Denise, for example, had not had prior opportunities to learn to use communication and information technologies, in either the minimal sense of 'learning how to drive them' or in the more culturally embedded sense of having incorporated them meaningfully into her own routines. Under these conditions, several things can happen. Often, classroom applications of new technologies remain at the level of the 'obvious'—you do presentations because that is what the machine and its software suggest are the kind of thing to do. It seems, however, that when it comes to integrating new technologies into curriculum, only certain activities appear 'obvious'. Moreover, these obvious things are often not the 'high value-adding' applications that serve learners well beyond school. Alternatively, learning opportunities with new technologies remain very much at the level of the operational dimension. This was apparent at both Tipping and Danton. None of the episodes we observed there—or, for that matter, practically anywhere in the entire project other than Abbotsdale—engaged students in exploring the cultural meanings of computer-mediated literacy practices, although at least in the case of Danton this could not reasonably have been expected, given the extracurricular nature of the project. Nor did the activities we observed emphasise the importance of students adopting critical stances towards information or the uses of new technologies in everyday social practices.

Third, when learning takes place under difficult conditions we should not be surprised if participants come away with less than optimal, and possibly hazy or confused, understandings of social practice. How we come to understand technology-mediated practices, and how we integrate new technologies into literacy-mediated practices, will depend on what we encounter in the way of practice—wherever and whenever we encounter it. Whatever our intentions as teachers may be, for instance, about 'covering' each of the operational, cultural and critical dimensions of literacy within our programs and relating them to each other as integral aspects of literacy, it is how literacy practices are experienced by learners that really matters. If they do not in fact experience the cultural and critical dimensions, they cannot be expected to take them seriously as integral to literacy.

What is experienced under difficult conditions has an important impact on what the social practice is seen to comprise—and, hence, what 'it' is learned as. We see this clearly at Danton: on one hand, Denise's initiative introduced students to a use of presentation software that at least resembles mainstream uses in 'authentic' business and commercial contexts. To this extent, she transcended the tendency to sublimate new technologies to processes of 'doing school'. Further, she enabled learners to see some of what is around and how it works at a basic operational level. On the other hand, participation in activities was seriously fragmented on account of time. Students were not involved in framing the generic template for the speech night HyperCard presentation. Tasks were subsequently delegated to individuals and small groups, somewhat like an assembly line. While students were being provided with opportunities they might not otherwise have had, to learn operational aspects of various technologies and applications (for example, using digital cameras, saving video grabs and inserting them into relevant sections of the presentation), they were not really being initiated into practices of producing presentations as a whole. They were not learning the skills as meaningful, coherent, integrated cultural practices, where critical judgments have to be made and a sense of the significance of the practice to social life achieved—all as a basis for being able to participate in it effectively. This, of course, is typical of much learning, whether in school or other educational institutions.

Under the conditions operating, it would have been unreasonable to expect any more than was achieved. At the same time, the issue prompts tough questions. At what point does the value and benefit of 'offering students opportunities to work with new technology applications' become outweighed by the risks of apprenticing them to less than optimal versions of social practice? It is important that departmental policies ensure follow-through, and not 'set schools up', leaving French lessons to fall over for want of RAM or for want of sufficient teacher experience and expertise to underwrite good-quality learning experiences.

3   Carlisle Primary: using multimedia in a multicultural setting

Carlisle Primary is a P–6 school serving a culturally diverse community of more than 30 nationalities in a large Australian metropolis. Vietnamese, Chinese, Khmers and Serbs form the largest groups. Over 90 per cent of the student population come from language backgrounds other than English. Unemployment is around 40 per cent in the school community, and 30–35 per cent of the population is transient. There are 22 students in the Year 2 class. Their teacher, John, has nine years' teaching experience and a strong commitment to finding effective ways for students to use computer information technologies to gather and present information. The class has access to two stand-alone computers (a Macintosh Performa 580CD and a Performa 400) with multimedia capacity but no internet connection. The software used includes ClarisWorks for drawing and graphics, KidPix Studio for multimedia, MS Word and PowerPoint, a range of drill-and-skill, problem-solving and popular games software, and some specialised basic literacy instruction programs, including the currently popular Wiggleworks.

Teaching and learning objectives involve a combination of specific literacy purposes, English language enhancement, general process aims, and technological proficiency goals. The class is studying the narrative genre of stories (genre-based learning figures strongly in the state's English language syllabus). The 'learning together' ethos of the class involves collaborative text (story) production in pairs or small groups. Students are involved in mastering word-processing, sound and graphics applications, and presentation software skills, as well as conventional print-based skills like handwriting and sketching. Underpinning the pedagogy are the aims that students progressively learn how new technologies provide access to different ways of writing, reading and investigating, how to transfer skills from one platform to another, and how to 'read' all of the media, making use of pictures, sound, text and video.

The activities involve pairs or groups producing multimedia presentations of stories. In one activity they construct a story of their own. In others, each pair works on jointly constructed retellings of a single page from a range of popular children's folk tales. In a characteristic sequence of lessons, students would create multi-panel storyboard formats on paper, roughing out ideas in pen, paper and crayon, then move on to using drawing, painting and sound applications on the computers to produce the finished slides. As final outcomes, the individual pages are assembled as slide-show presentations of the retold stories, using text, graphics and sound.

In a typical instance, a pair of boys works on their presentation of one of the folk tales, recording multiple 'takes' of their text. After the first take, they discover they have selected the 'no-sound' option on each slide. At the second take, the sound is too soft. Two girls work on a story about dinosaurs. They have prepared a narrative using an eight-panel storyboard, roughing out their text and illustrations on paper. Using this draft, they prepare slides for their final presentation using drawing and painting tools in KidPix. They draw a purple dinosaur with a red mouth, then delete and retrieve it several times in the process of finally changing its colour to yellow. They complete the slide by keying in 'Andrea's Dinosaur' by Andrea and Mai. During the draft production phase John works with students, discussing their illustrations and texts and helping them clarify their intentions.

The Year 5/6 class has 30 students, 19 of whom are in Year 5 and 11 in Year 6. Ninety per cent are from language backgrounds other than English and ten students have been in Australia less than six months. Their teacher, Kate, is doing a master's degree in technology and literacy. She coordinates the school's literacy learning team. She is at ease using new technologies in her teaching and has a positive view of her current levels of understanding. Kate sees her role in the classroom as facilitator of independent and self-directed, cooperative learners, and expresses great enthusiasm for promoting divergent thinking processes. In her view, new technologies will be an integral part of students' future lives as evolving technologies promote life-long learning. She speaks of her commitment to developing students' advanced reading strategies, such as skimming and scanning. Kate places great importance on information skills. She describes literacy as more than reading and writing—students need explicit instruction in new information technologies.

The school is determined to ensure all students are equipped to succeed in the information age. Every class has a computer and each grade level a shared multimedia computer. The Year 5/6 classroom set-up is the norm: a Macintosh Performa 580CD with a Stylewriter 1200 printer sits under the chalkboard. A second Mac (LC II with colour monitor) is wheeled out from the storeroom each morning. The computers are available to students before school and at lunchtime. Students can also access a Mac laptop, two old PC laptops with printers and a multimedia computer in the library, where there is an internet connection.

Access to the computers in class is self-regulated, although Kate ensures all students have access and a variety of software, including: ClarisWorks, MS Word, KidPix Studio, Corel Draw 5, Excel, MS PowerPoint and Solitaire.

As the day begins, Kate quickly gives instructions about tasks to be completed. Included is the invitation to use the Mac for work that needs to be published. At the 'publishing centre', in another part of the room, a girl is using ClarisWorks to publish her report on the environment—part of the contract on which she is working. She has drafted it on paper and conferenced with a peer. She chooses a font then calls to Kate, who does not hear. Another girl comes over to help and they speak in their shared language. By the end of the lesson, she has finished a page using a handwriting font and the copy-and-paste facilities. As she finishes at the computer, another girl takes her place.

Meanwhile, three boys work on the Mac Performa creating a slide show using KidPix. This is how they have decided to report what they have understood from a unit of work on environment. They develop ideas, decide on the presentation, and do the editing as they go along. Two boys decide to construct a creature using ClipArt body parts. They are seeking a magic effect as the creature waves a wand over the garbage bin. The boys want a 'ding' sound to signify a magic spell, and take turns at recording their voices 'dinging'. When they cannot find a ClipArt picture of a rubbish tin, Kate says they will have to draw one. They do, then write on the screen 'Ka boom!!! Like this one'—recording one boy saying 'Ka boom' (after much practice) and the others adding 'Like this one'. After much experimenting, they save their graphics and signs and arrange the slides they have as a slide show, choosing a variety of transitions, a prerecorded sound for the flower growing, and recorded sounds for the sun ('phew') and the flower ('wow'). The flower grows bigger as the sun's rays strike it. Kate asks how many slides they have and how many they need for the entire show. They say they need one more. When she asks if they have planned it out, one of the boys shakes his head. They then produce the final slide using a ClipArt koala, adding, 'We hope you have learned something'.

The student activities in this vignette contrast markedly with other activities based on Kate's avowed aim to make teaching explicit and to use theoretically based organisers like Bloom's (1956) Taxonomy and Gardner's (1993) Multiple Intelligences to guide the pedagogy. Elsewhere, three girls explain that Kate has negotiated the 'Environment' topic with the class and set them to designing their own unit (in this case around Bloom's Taxonomy, with requirements tailored to individual student ability). These girls tell us that they have had to design and undertake five activities in the areas of knowledge and comprehension, four in application, two in analysis, two in synthesis and two in evaluation. They negotiated the activities as a group and then with the teacher to ensure all facets had been covered. A mix of individual and group work is involved.

The procedure requires that at the end of the unit all students produce their work in 'an appropriate format', to be decided by each student. Decisions vary widely. Some are producing fully illustrated folders in the shapes of various Australian fauna, one is producing a concertina-like display board which folds into the shape of a flying fox, while yet another is constructing a replica worm farm into which work samples are being placed. Others are producing multimedia presentations, using KidPix and ClarisWorks slide shows. Most written work is word-processed.

These brief portraits of practice at Carlisle exemplify a great deal of what we saw across the sites in general. There is ample evidence of great enthusiasm for and enjoyment in learning, and a sense of comfort, achievement and confidence on the part of learners around a range of new technologies. One student reports that most school work employs computers and that Kate wants them to learn how to use the computer 'all by ourselves without any help', and to explore assistance provided by the medium itself. 'At home', says another boy, 'I just open the computer up and look around. That's how I learn. I teach myself'. Students who had used computers at Carlisle since Kindergarten were confident and sure in their operational abilities, and believed they would become more proficient with further practice. On the other hand, some of the cases alert us to issues that are worth close consideration.

First, it is important to ensure that the important cultural dimension of literacy is not overwhelmed by operational considerations. Throughout the sites in general we found genres like narratives, information reports, projects and the like serving mainly as vehicles for introducing students to specific software applications. It is important that learning these applications not be detached from understanding the meanings of the practices which are mediated by digital text production, and from notions of what is included in and/or written out of the practice. Some of the matters germane to the cultural dimension could be considered by having learners reflect on assumptions and values that come with slide-show templates or, indeed, with the production of presentation software itself—and how these relate to the practices they are currently involved in. In cases like the slide show on Environment, it is not really clear what the major literacy attainments are for the group of boys in question. What generic practice has been engaged in here? To what extent are learnings like 'planning it' actually more important than learning to drive slide-show and other multimedia applications? How can we best integrate cultural and critical dimensions into this kind of work in conjunction with operational aspects?

Second, some of the practices raise the question of what counts as effective learning involving new technologies. If we believe that effective learning connects what learners do now 'in meaningful and motivating ways with "mature" (insider) versions of related social practices, and with what they will be doing at later points in their life trajectories' (Gee, Hull & Lankshear 1996: 4), we might consider whether the same software applications can be taught via practices that are closer to those employed by expert users of presentation software and the internet. If there are, in fact, established practices of using presentation software and webpages as a medium for rewriting children's stories, recognising this and making the connection between the classroom activity and the use of language in an established domain of human activity will become an important part of the learning. If there are not, the criteria for effective learning will be better served by trying to attach the use of the new technologies to more lifelike and real-life applications.

Third, we can revisit the 'old wine in new bottles' syndrome in relation to the question of what is going to count as effective literacy in the information age. There is no doubt that the teachers in the study were convinced that the information age and the wide-scale incorporation of new communication and information technologies into daily routines ups the ante for literacy in many ways. This insight, however, sometimes came into conflict with the practices actually engaged in. There was a recognition that somehow the 'age' had changed: we were in some other age previously, but today's learners are inhabiting the information age. In chapter 2, we raised the question of what this means in relation to literacy and literacy education. Among other things, it means learning how to generate, retrieve, evaluate, process, manage, relate, refine and present information in ways that have currency in everyday social practices. The enormity and difficulty of the challenge involved in understanding and anticipating these practices and adapting them to meaningful classroom activities should not be underestimated. It represents a major task, and when we look to many teacher education programs in literacy and technology we find they have not even begun to tackle the issue seriously.

The fact remains that we often find in classrooms practices that are based in the past rather than looking to the present and to the future. We find, for example, a lot of 1970s- and 80s-style process writing and conventional practices of children's literature being harnessed to new technologies. For all the literary merit these practices may have, information-based practices occupy a different space. We need to seek a balance between these different 'spaces'. Once again, this is by no means a challenge for teachers alone. If we are to tackle the information age in classroom learning, it is important that teacher education, curriculum development, literacy and technology research, and policy initiatives play their part, together with teachers in their own professional development, in working out what this means in practice and in theory.

4 Tech High: two vignettes

Tech High began in 1991 as the first purpose-built technology high school in the state. Located in a rapidly growing middle-class suburb, it serves a population where 40 per cent of the people come from language backgrounds other than English. Students from 48 different linguistic communities attend the school. Cantonese and Mandarin form the largest foreign language groups. Originally built for 850 students, at the time of our visit the school had a roll of more than 1200. Janine, teacher of the years 7 and 8 classes, is in her third year of teaching English. She sees herself as 'of the computer generation' and feels comfortable using computers for lesson preparation, administrative tasks and teaching. Her classes comprise 25–28 male and female students. A school survey indicates that 85 per cent of students have home computer access and 35 per cent have home internet access. At school, students have access to desktop computers—typically, upgraded 386 machines—in computer labs, as well as to class sets of laptops running external disk drives. The main software packages used in the lessons observed are word-processing, publishing and graphics packages, including AmiPro.

Janine defines her general teaching aims in terms of 'helping kids to develop their own skills in literacy, reading, writing and media'. She also places high priority on the fact that use of computers heightens students' awareness of presentation aspects of their work—referring to student work displayed on the classroom walls with great satisfaction. Her more specific aims in the lessons observed are to introduce Year 7 students to the genre of newspaper reports involving both stories and illustrations, and to engage Year 8 students in the main aspects of playwriting.

The students in the Year 7 class work in groups of four or five in the computer lab. Their assignment, designed to take two to three weeks, is to compile a four-page newspaper built around stories to do with the school. Given the size of the groups, the teacher recommends that one or two students do the 'typing', while the others write new articles using AmiPro, which allows text production in columns and has a graphics menu where students look for illustrations for their articles. Students write drafts in their English books before keying them into the computer. A typical snapshot involves two students working on writing articles while two enter stories from handwritten copy, editing as they go and using the spell-check before printing out.

The Year 8 class works in the English home room using the laptops—also in groups of four or five—producing five-minute plays to perform before the class. One or two students per group key in material while others dictate dialogue, design costumes, sketch characters on sheets of paper, and construct simple props and costume items. Roles switch when members feel like a change. Although tasks are always divided up, the groups maintain themselves as 'wholes', discussing plot or character development as they go about their respective tasks. When a member has something to add to the text, s/he momentarily takes over the keyboard, making the addition—sometimes signalling a transition in roles.

Two related issues are worth reiterating briefly here. The first has to do with effective learning. If we accept that what learners do now should be linked to what they will do later and elsewhere as they arc their way through trajectories of active participation in social institutions and practices, it is important that school learning be as faithful as possible to the social practices to which they are intended to relate. This has some important implications for classroom activities such as creating and publishing newspaper stories. It will be important to attend to matters of layout and illustrating stories. There will, however, be other important aspects of 'mature' versions of journalism as social practice to be taken into account.

These will range from finding ways to establish an editorial policy and slant for the newspaper, to imitating real-life procedures for illustrating stories (taking photographs as opposed to locating graphics in preset menus) and real-life journalist roles (cadet reporter, senior reporter, page or section editor, subeditors), and observing 'authentic' editing procedures, structures of decision-making and editorial power. What, for example, would be involved in dealing with the cultural and critical dimensions of 'writing newspaper stories', in addition to the operational dimension construed as word-processing and graphics applications?

The second issue concerns the meaningfulness of the roles assigned to computers in classroom practices and the consequences of the roles that are assigned to them for how the practices/literacies get constructed in class. In the example of writing short plays it may be an open question as to whether there is any need to employ a computer. Is it possible that the social practice/literacy of play-writing might actually be better represented and learned by leaving the computer out of it altogether? This is especially important if the availability of laptops means that learning the role of playwright gets disturbed by having to turn it into a group activity involving turn-taking on a computer. Playwriting is a distinctive cultural practice and literacy. If the point of having playwriting in English is to initiate learners into the cultural dimension of playwriting, it is risky to give computers the power to override an initiation that is faithful to the culture of the practice. To the extent that the 'reluctant uptakers' at Ealing have these sorts of considerations in mind when they express fears about a focus on new technologies taking the emphasis away from what they see as the real business of English, they have a valid point.

Elmwood: gardening for literacy

Elmwood High is a large school located in a mainly middle-class outer suburb of a state capital. The Year 9 Agri-Technology class has 32 students: 18 girls, 14 boys, almost entirely Australian-born, native English speakers. Their teacher, Victor, has been teaching for twenty years, and was asked by the school in 1995 to work as part of a team to set up a technology department in line with the emergence of Technology as a Key Learning Area.

This portrait is the odd one out in the entire study. There is not a computer to be found. Victor and the students are engaged in the 'Garden Project', which involves a rich array of literacy activities intrinsic to the 'design, make and appraise' conception of the KLA Technology. The most 'sophisticated' literacy tool to be found at any point of the project is the overhead projector, which students used in reporting their work to the class at the end of the process.

The 'Garden Project' is presented to students as a carefully 'scaffolded' activity which is structured and organised by an elaborate set of worksheets. These are arranged in sequence in piles, and at the outset of the project the students are asked to collect one copy of each in the order laid out. The sheets fall into two categories: information sheets, which will guide students' work throughout the project, and activity sheets to be completed by the students. The project involves designing, making and appraising a home garden which can be developed in pots, as a hydroponic type, or as a conventional garden bed. The main consideration is that the garden accords with home and family needs and circumstances. Victor requires the students to undertake the project at home, after discussion and negotiation with parents, as he prefers his school-based learning activities to approximate as closely as possible 'real-life' situations and practices in the world beyond school. Many students find the negotiations the most challenging part of the project.

While Victor claims no knowledge of Elmwood's English program or policy, the project is also a context for learning and practising language and literacy along the lines of the state's P–10 English syllabus. At the time of our visit, Victor was teaching a unit of work that at the level of formal intent is often exemplary in its approach and contribution to language and literacy education across the curriculum. Scaffolded oral and written tasks and the worksheets, together with Victor's oral instructions in classroom lessons, highlight, model and make explicit the generic structure of reports, as well as procedures associated with technological productions and practices. Attempts to relate text to context, enact 'authentic' social purposes and approximate 'real-life' and lifelike practices within language and literacy education are often hampered by the narrow, text-based character of school subjects. Subjects like Agri-Technology, which have long been grounded in close relations with the world of work and domestic productive activity, have good potential to approximate these ideals in school-based learning. This potential is very evident in the project.

The 'Garden Project' involves a wide range of language and literacy practices, oral and written, to be undertaken in class and at home. These include negotiations about the kind of garden to be constructed, talking and thinking around the design of the project with those whose interests are directly involved, and considering the balance between budget requirements and what the garden would yield—an 'authentic' consideration if ever there was one. Students undertake these negotiations and deliberations with the assistance of carefully structured procedures for identifying the relevant factors, assigning weight to them, identifying the plus and minus aspects of particular options and keeping a careful record of these. Victor's expressed purpose here is to engage students in setting about the process the way 'real practitioners' do in 'real life', and he draws on his personal and professional involvement in these ways of real practitioners in developing carefully scaffolded tasks. Students complete a range of worksheets, maintain a diary, and give an oral presentation based on the model of a formal conference report of work undertaken or in the vein of a seminar designed to 'sell' a particular product or approach. Students are coached in the development of props, in how to deliver the presentation, how and when to use overheads, charts and handouts. At the end of the procedure they have, in addition to their 'literate record' of the project, a real-life material product—a garden of some kind or another—which represents the application of a design–make–appraise sequence, and which has embedded explicit forms and processes of language and literacy.

Elmwood provides a fascinating perspective on the literacy—technology interface as well as an interesting and important perspective from which to consider the literacy–technology challenge. Five issues in particular stand out, and they provide an illuminating end to this chapter.

First, school-based language and literacy practices are often constrained within discrete subject areas, when they can and should be extended across the curriculum in ways that add value though appropriate transfer of knowledge and competence. For example, some of Victor's generic literacies within KLA Technology could be extended, so that within subject Science students do more than simply follow prepackaged and formulaic science programs based on textbooks or their equivalent.

Second, school literacies, and the practices in which they are embedded, often impede prospects for effective learning by focusing too narrowly on the child and on the classroom walls or school gate as defining the parameters of school learning. This often results in what is commonly referred to as 'doing school', in which students are required to engage in practices that have either no place or a strictly limited place beyond the school context. There are two important questions for language and literacy education here. The first asks: What is the desirable relationship between school and out-of-school literacies and related practices? The second is contingent on the first: If there should be significant articulation between school practices and wider Discourses (Gee 1996), how well are classroom practices measuring up?

Third, there was much potential for developing the cultural and critical dimensions of literacy at Elmwood as a consequence of literacy activity being grounded to the extent that it genuinely approximated to materially based 'real-life' and lifelike practices. The various literacy tasks could readily be perceived as intrinsic components of technology as cultural practice. And ample scope exists for the critical dimension of literacy in undertakings like the Garden Project as engaging in critique (why do/write/record it this way rather than that?) has an explicit, concrete and objective point and purpose. There is a material 'bottom line' relating to felt interests, available resources, tangible returns on investment of time, commitment, and money.

Fourth, Elmwood provides a valuable corrective to our largely commodified notions of technology as electronic gadgets and 'whizzbangery' that provide solutions to problems—including educational problems—and allegedly hold the key to social progress. This kind of thinking suits producers and distributors of high-technology products and often proves expeditious for policy-makers and politicians. At this time, Australian schools are under almost unassailable pressure to join the hi-tech race, and in doing so risk becoming caught in mystified thinking about what tools can and cannot do. Tools on their own cannot design, make and appraise. They can, however, be powerful and effective adjuncts to designing, making and appraising, in the hands of competent technology practitioners. Elmwood demonstrates the importance, particularly for resource-strapped schools, of thinking about technology and literacy from a perspective wider than the application of 'up-to-the-minute electronic technologies'.

Finally, (literacy) pedagogy at Elmwood was not driven by a particular technology. The distinctive 'technoliteracy' of the Garden Project—a literacy embedded in a particular mode and domain of technological practice—was not forced into a distorted mould as the price to be paid for 'having to fit a computer into it somehow or other'. The outcome was a rich opportunity for students to experience the character and efficacy of literacy as an embedded dimension of an 'authentic' kind of social practice. If this is what literacy education should be about—as we believe it is—then Elmwood provides a helpful corrective to current, coerced temptations to put technological carts before literacy horses. More importantly, it provides us with a benchmark for assessing our integration of new technologies into literacy education: How and when does it make sense to include which and what new technologies, for what ends, and with what outcomes?

In chapter 5 we suggest a framework of ideas and principles for practice we find useful for thinking about what we found in the study sites and for deciding how to confront this crucial educational question.

5

Patterns and principles of classroom practice

In chapters 1 and 4 we describe some educationally illuminating aspects of literacy and technology practice drawn from a broad range of primary and secondary school classrooms. We also identify some of the key issues and themes arising from our interpretations of what we saw, read and were told. Although we have tried to avoid overlap in our accounts, it should be apparent that many of the things going on in particular classrooms show up in others—even if, at first glance, they appear to be different.

Common to nearly all the classrooms was a commitment to and enthusiasm for drawing a range of new technologies into literacy education activities. We found evidence everywhere of energy, hard work and perseverance—often in the face of considerable odds—and a cheerful determination to construct purposeful activities involving new technologies. We were also impressed by the efforts teachers made in looking for ways to make things work and, in some cases, to overcome trepidation born of inexperience, using whatever human resources were available to get assistance and to go forward. However, as our intention is to contribute something of value to enhance school and classroom approaches to literacy and technology education, we have tended to highlight the aspects of practice we think can provide helpful clues as to how the task might be done more effectively. If we have paid less attention to the enthusiasm, energy and commitment than we have to aspects that provide useful leads for enhancing practice, it has not been with a view to downplaying what schools and teachers are already doing but to offer grounded suggestions for how we might progress from here.

To provide a foundation for advancing the practical suggestions presented in chapter 6, it is necessary to look again at the site studies to identify the patterns that emerged from our analysis. Overall, we identify five broad patterns of practice, added here to those identified in the original project (Digital Rhetorics 1999; Lankshear et al. 1997). These patterns were highly suggestive of a set of five general principles for guiding practice—principles that we believe should underpin and inform ongoing efforts to improve literacy education in an age where information and communication practices are increasingly mediated by digital electronic technologies. The patterns and principles have been developed to take into account as far as possible the issues identified in earlier chapters.

FIVE PATTERNS OF CLASSROOM PRACTICE

We see five significant patterns evident overall in the practices described in earlier chapters. They are not found across all the individual sites, although they tend to be present to a greater or lesser extent in most—particularly when schools as a whole, rather than selected classrooms, are considered. In several cases the classrooms chosen for study were atypical of their larger school contexts: they were the ones known to be using new technologies on a regular basis. The five patterns, inherent in practice, are:

- complexity;
- fragility;
- discontinuity;
- conservation;
- limited authenticity.

In describing these five patterns, we also consider some of the important issues and implications associated with them. Our analysis of the patterns suggests helpful principles for developing ideas, strategies and approaches to enhance classroom practice at the literacy–technology interface.

Complexity

Classrooms are complex, in the sense of having a large number of interrelating components operating within and beyond them.

However, in describing classrooms as complex, we are doing more than simply pointing to their obvious state: we are also pointing to ideas that derive from an emerging field of knowledge known as 'complexity theory' (Waldrop 1992). Viewed from this perspective, classrooms are complex, self-organising, adaptive systems: they have to arrange themselves around the interactions between their various human and non-human components. Each time a new component— such as a new technology or a new policy—is added, it does not feed one more 'thing' into the mix in a linear way: rather, its introduction produces a compound effect. The new component rearranges all the other interactions, and may add many more in its own right. Classroom practices then have to reorganise themselves around this new complexity, which involves changes in roles, changes in relationships, changes in patterns of work and changes in allocations of space in the classroom.

When we add an internet connection, for instance, it brings with it into the classroom a whole new set of agents—remote computers, students and teachers in other parts of the world—all of which affect, in complex and often unpredictable ways, what occurs. Involvement in projects with groups elsewhere changes the nature of classroom projects profoundly. It is no longer simply a matter of adapting to local conditions, as was often the case when print prevailed. Now classrooms have to take account of different cultural ways of interacting, become culturally sensitive, handle language differences, understand ranges of experience and world views, and deal with various technical complications such as managing telecommunications links.

The idea that the classroom is a complex system—in which all the components negotiate their roles with all the other components, in which the teacher is just one of a complex array of agents, and in which the outcomes are self-organising—is an idea still relatively unfamiliar to teachers (Bigum 1997). This understanding of classrooms tells us that complexity is not something to combat, as it cannot be removed, but is something to be lived with. At the same time, it offers the notion of negotiation as a watchword for developing strategies that enhance the quality of learning outcomes.

The idea of 'negotiation' among elements in a classroom overrides traditional conceptions of classrooms as either teacher-centred or student-centred. The kind of negotiation informed by an understanding of classroom complexity involves much more than giving some authority and agency over to students to take care of technical aspects of computing that are beyond the teacher's knowledge—it becomes an entire 'mindset': a way of teachers going about their business and perceiving the roles and modes of operation of other agents in the classroom (Bigum 1997).

To take an example, a teacher may have certain ideas about how much noise or movement is tolerable in her classroom. These guide the kinds of activities and social learning groups she encourages and tries to build. And these activities and groupings may or may not work, depending on how other components 'play their hand'. A teacher's success depends very much on how adept she is at negotiating technologies that are less compliant than students and often less amenable to 'correction'. Her success also depends on how skilful she is at negotiating with students, who are often more 'clued up' than teachers in 'assigning roles' to new technologies—some of which may be subversive and disruptive.

Whether we are talking about technologised classrooms or not, 'complexity' gives teachers useful ways of thinking about many of the classic problems associated with their work. For instance, from the standpoint of complexity, we do not see developments using new technologies as mere 'add-ons' to classroom life. By contrast, we see new technologies as active 'participants' in the system, which are as capable of forming powerful liaisons with learners as they are with teachers.

A further aspect of complexity involves the fact that new communication and information technologies can project learning into more globalised contexts. In the past, learning assignments that had international scope and significance tended to be adapted to local circumstances. Today, schools at the local level can become joint collaborators with their counterparts from all over the world. Boundaries between states and nations get broken down and become less relevant. Correspondingly, teachers and students have to learn to see themselves as participants in much wider and more complicated learning communities than before. Successful negotiations of roles in these larger, self-organising systems call for deeper forms of understanding, awareness and sensitivity—cultural, social, ethical—than in the past. This has important implications for preservice and in-service teacher education, professional development programs, and school-based teaching enrichment initiatives.

Fragility

To be effective, the components of self-organising systems such as classrooms must assign roles successfully among themselves. When a component is unable to play its role in a classroom—whether it is a teacher, a student, a computer, a modem or a phone line—it is unlikely that the classroom will be able to reorganise in a way that allows computer use to continue in curriculum work, at least in the short run. Classrooms are especially sensitive to the loss of certain components, such as an expert teacher, a key support person, an essential piece of software or a phone connection. Fragility was woven deeply into the fabric of practice in several classrooms, exacerbated in some cases by the norm of teacher-centred curriculum and pedagogy. Many of our site studies focused on issues and implications arising from technical aspects of fragility: difficulties accessing the internet and difficulties getting enough technical support to keep things running. We also found non-technical examples of fragility related to restricted or underdeveloped professional knowledge and understanding of how to integrate new technologies meaningfully and transparently into learning activities.

Acknowledging and tackling problems of fragility assume major importance when new technologies are used in literacy education. In most of the sites investigated, we found new technology initiatives dependent on a few individuals—sometimes only one or two. Successful practice, however, relies on access to technological support, as well as on teacher enthusiasm and a disposition for self-activated learning (for example, developing do-it-yourself expertise). As in any system, a new 'technologies in learning' project needs close attention at the technical, servicing and upgrade levels. It is necessary, therefore, to have capable people acting in these support roles. But if fragility is to be confronted in reliable and lasting ways, it is important to make the capability base as wide as possible. Schools need to avoid locking up expertise in a few hands, as this generates dependence and inequity. The ideal is to implement cross-curriculum and whole-school initiatives—to build a culture of expertise and commitment. It is also vital to pursue a balance between the options taken up and the availability of resources to service those options.

The issue of fragility suggests an important location for policy development at the school level. In a minority of the sites we visited, school policies were formulated to help tackle fragility by making new technology initiatives not person-dependent but cross-curriculum, involving all staff members. But we need to remember that, while some schools can instigate reforms assured of ongoing resources for their funding, many have extremely limited options (Secada 1989). Schools in the latter category need to keep the issue uppermost in the minds of their professional association lobbyists and state department liaison personnel, as well as on the agendas of their school boards and decision-making bodies, which may otherwise, despite the best of intentions, commit the school to unsustainable initiatives.

Discontinuity

Effective learning programs call for continuity from point to point, as well as across individual components of programs. Continuity breaks down where, for example, students do computing-rich work on a regular basis one year and rarely get to use a new technology the next. Discontinuities can also arise where there is inadequate programming for scope and sequence, and where there are uneven concentrations of new technology resources—human and non-human—within schools and between schools. As schools and classrooms are complex systems, uneven concentrations of expertise and equipment are to be expected, and achieving more even distributions is not easy. Nonetheless, continuity must be pursued strategically, especially within a school and between local schools, including the transition from feeder primary to secondary schools.

In several of the sites we investigated our attention was drawn to concern that continuity was tenuous—especially from one year or grade level to the next. As a pattern of practice, discontinuity was inferred more than observed, because of the brief periods we spent in fieldwork. Teachers, however, expressed concern on a regular basis, and in only one school did we observe evidence of detailed, systematic, careful planning for curriculum continuity across all levels.

A further important and interesting facet of discontinuity is evident in policy development at the interface of literacy and new technologies. Individual policy statements—such as syllabus documents for English, statements and profiles for Key Learning Areas, and policies for the use of computers in schools and for teacher computing competencies—show few if any signs that they have been developed with systematic, collaborative input from personnel across the literacy–technology divide. Many of the literacy policy statements are uninformed about the role and place of new technologies in contemporary textual practices. Likewise, policies concerned with learning technologies rarely reflect input from people with strong subject knowledge or expertise in literacy. This continues traditional practices of subject 'compartmentalising' and resonates with earlier failures to generate effective across-the-curriculum approaches to literacy. Failure to practise and model continuity within policy development is likely only to exacerbate problems of continuity at the level of classroom practice.

Identifying ways to make continuity as robust as possible is a major consideration when schools make curriculum policy decisions. Students benefit when the school's technology policy is coherent, comprehensive and well integrated with other relevant policies— particularly its literacy policy. Hence, it is important to build broad-based policy development teams and to develop such policies in conjunction with each other.

Continuity within the school—from grade to grade and across subject areas—is easier to ensure when most staff use new technologies in the classroom. Conversely, continuity is difficult to achieve when participation and the distribution of resources and expertise are uneven. Of course, from the perspective of understanding schools and classrooms as complex systems, localised concentrations of knowledge and equipment are to be expected, and even under the best of conditions achieving and maintaining even distributions is difficult. It has to be worked at continually, and built into recruitment policies, incentives and professional development activity. The same applies to efforts by schools in an area to maximise continuity with their feeder schools and vice versa, as well as with sociocultural practices and socioeconomic conditions operating in their communities.

Aspects of continuity between primary and secondary schools and between schools and homes are significant here. Restricted availability of computers influences how they are used. In the primary-school classrooms we observed learners often enjoyed considerable autonomy over how, when and why computers were used. Students in high schools have much less autonomy. Students with access to home computers can continue learning in 'play' or 'acquisition' environments (Gee 1991), and can make decisions on important matters: with whom, for how long, what and how. They can experiment, explore and immerse themselves in the environment, learning the language and culture of the space, as well as learning the skills necessary to participate. It is interesting to compare the home and school as two self-organising systems and inquire about the roles of the various agents in both settings. The learnings that occur in the two settings are likely to be markedly different. Those with access only at school may learn that computers are only for particular tasks—for the final copy of a report or constructing a database in history: that is, for a school task, an intellectual exercise with little relevance to the outside world.

Conservation

There was a strong pattern of practice across most sites that involved 'conserving' familiar forms and routines of literacy education, and making the use of new technologies 'accommodate' these familiar forms and routines—the 'new wine in old bottles' syndrome (Lankshear & Bigum, in press). Teachers often seemed to identify technological applications that resonated with their pedagogical styles and that fitted new technologies into classroom business as usual. Much of what we saw could be described as routine school literacy with new technologies added here and there.

A lot of what we observed amounted to 1970s or 80s process writing (draft, confer, redraft, confer, publish the final copy) reclothed in electronic garb, and a traditional, print-based approach to children's and adolescents' literature with a digital make-over. Long-established classroom language and literacy education routines were now being undertaken as slide-show and webpage presentations, rather than as literal 'cuttings' from print resources, followed by literal 'pastings' into workbooks. The final format is all that had changed. Many practices, indeed probably the majority of those observed, were quintessentially 'school-like' in structure and content, the main difference being that they had been 'technologised'.

As we point out in chapter 1, our site studies largely affirm Seymour Papert's (1993) observation that time travellers from the 19th century could step into a contemporary classroom and know at a glance where they were. They also affirm Steven Hodas' (1996) arguments about the capacity of classrooms to shape successive technologies to familiar classroom forms. Hodas makes the point that the role of the school as a 'defining technology', and even as a 'determining technology', influences the ways in which other technologies—in our case, new communication and information technologies—get taken up. It is important to recognise that school is a technology: a way of doing things or of getting things done. Indeed, the school is a powerful and well-established technology. Not surprisingly, its customary ways of doing things—of doing the business of educating children—confront head-on whatever 'contributory' technologies are introduced into the larger 'school technology'. This often results in precisely what we saw—the forced accommodation of new technologies to classroom 'logics' in ways that severely limited their potential applications.

From a historical perspective, the accommodation of communication and information technologies to familiar routines—even routines that may seem 'odd', 'inefficient', 'wasteful' or 'misguided' to expert users—is not necessarily a bad thing (see Marvin 1988). The car, after all, was originally conceived as a horseless carriage. It becomes problematic, however, when such practices are cast as 'authentic'. As we note in chapter 2, this can amount to teachers and students gaining opportunities to learn how to use particular new technology applications with greater mechanical fluency, at the cost of giving students—especially those who have direct access out of school to all manner of 'authentic' practices involving new technologies—inferior learning experiences.

If we believe that school learning is to prepare learners for more than participation in distinctively school Discourses (Gee 1996), we need to be aware of the school as a defining technology. We need to consider how this influences the uptake of any technology—from pencils to PowerPoint—in the classroom, and to consider means for making learning activities as 'real' as possible.

Limited authenticity

The pattern of 'conservation' needs to be considered in conjunction with the pattern we refer to here as 'limited authenticity'. The issue of authenticity has to do with the relationship between school or school-like practices and social practices in the world beyond school. It also has to do with questions about what counts as effective learning and what school learning is for (Gee, Hull & Lankshear 1996). In short, it concerns the relationship between school and the rest of the world, and the role of school learning in relation to the world at large.

If we look at the ways people use new technologies in 'mature' versions of social practice in the world beyond school (for example, in work, leisure, civic life) and think of these as 'authentic', we are forced to conclude that many uses made of new technologies in the sites we observed have limited authenticity. The issue at stake here is recognised in various education policy and syllabus statements by reference to such distinctions as 'focused learning' or 'direct-teaching' episodes, 'lifelike' teaching and learning activities, and 'real-life' teaching and learning activities (see Queensland P–10 English syllabus). The 'Garden Project' described in chapter 4, which involved no use of new technologies, was as close as any of the practices came to resembling 'real life'. Some were more or less 'lifelike'—for instance, the idea of producing posters for the film premiere, and generating a slide show to illustrate a speech. Others that we might think to be lifelike because they are 'versions' of 'authentic' practices—such as producing school newspapers—appear less lifelike when the differences between the school-based practice and 'the real thing' are considered. In further cases, such as having students produce retellings of stories as slide shows, the connections to 'real-life' practices are remote. It may be better to think of such activities as focused-learning episodes, where the emphasis is on operational aspects of 'driving' a piece of software and English language acquisition rather than on the authenticity of the activity, as an approximation to how people engage social practice in 'real life'.

We are at a historical juncture, where many people are asking anew the question: What are schools for? Recent answers have included: better preparation for the world of work; to ensure that all learners get enough literacy to participate in school; to develop self-sufficient and responsible citizens; and to enable learners to function effectively as adults in the future. As Robertson (1998) observes in her analysis of the corporatisation of Canada's schools, some of the answers that have been provided are ones teachers would want to stay well clear of. Indeed, the findings from Robertson's investigative work (discussed in the preface to this book) provide the strongest possible incentive for teachers and citizens at large to revisit the question: What are schools for?

It is generally assumed that the learning done in schools will map onto social practices in the larger world: that participation in school-based Discourses will help prepare learners for successful participation in 'mature' versions of related Discourses in the 'real world' (Gee, Hull & Lankshear 1996). For example, for the school Discourse of woodwork, the related outside Discourse would be carpentry. However, for subjects like geography, history and science, the related outside Discourses are less clear. Are they the formal practices of being a historian or a scientist? Of being a teacher of history or science? Or of being an informed citizen or parent who can help the kids with their homework? For school Discourses of literacy, the presumed related outside Discourses would include the myriad literate practices embedded in everyday social practices— from writing notes to children and letters to families, to writing minutes of meetings and letters to editors, to communicating with banks and other businesses, to writing newspaper articles or books, and producing workplace memos.

A sociocultural perspective emphasises the fact that successful participation in a Discourse is more than a matter of becoming proficient at the 'operational' aspects of practices. There is a lot of appropriate cultural learning involved as well—values and beliefs, attitudes, ways of gesturing, dressing and speaking. This is the point at which relationships between school Discourses and outside Discourses become problematic. To a large extent, school learning is not embedded in 'mature' versions of outside social practices. It is embedded in characteristic school Discourses.

Whether we are dealing with the print world of learning mediated by pen or the digital world of learning mediated by new technologies, the question of 'authenticity' looms large. We need to clarify whether school learning is for 'participation in the school or classroom Discourse itself', or whether it is for 'learning Discourses outside school'. And if it is for outside Discourses, which ones, and 'what sort of relationship to these outside Discourses should or do school and classroom Discourses contract' (Gee, Hull & Lankshear 1996: 15)?

Whatever the answers to these questions are—and work like Robertson's (1998) demonstrates the risks involved in going for too much 'authenticity' without considering whose 'authentic' worlds and practices we are buying into—it is obvious that classroom activities should not risk unwittingly introducing learners to misunderstandings of social practices. The fact that teachers feel comfortable and proficient with new technologies may count for little if they lack knowledge of 'authentic' embeddings of the technological tools in 'mature' versions of social practice. If school learning practices are intended to begin the initiation of learners into 'mature' versions of outside social practices, the gap between them and the 'real thing' should not be too wide. And it certainly should not be counterproductive.

FIVE PRINCIPLES FOR CLASSROOM PRACTICE

We see five principles as particularly useful to guide the effective integration of new technologies into classroom-based literacy education. They are also useful to guide curriculum activity more broadly. We call these principles:

- teachers first;
- complementarity;
- workability;
- equity;
- focus on trajectories.

The first four of these principles are based on the work of Chris Bigum and Jane Kenway (1998). We describe the principles in turn, taking care to consider associated issues and implications.

Teachers first

'Teachers first' asserts the imperative to take account of the needs of teachers in learning new technologies and their relationship to literacy education, even before tackling the needs of students. The reasoning behind this principle is that for teachers to make informed educational choices about using new technologies in classroom practice, they must first know how to use them, and any benefits of doing so, for their own purposes. In other words, teachers need support in making use of new technologies to enhance their personal work before learning to use them in their teaching.

The teachers-first principle speaks directly to important elements of at least three of the patterns: complexity, discontinuity, and fragility. Indeed, teachers first is so obvious it is difficult to understand how education systems can be left to create patterns of fragility and discontinuity by projecting teachers into situations for which they have not been appropriately prepared. Part of the answer is that insufficient heed has been paid to a sociocultural perspective on literacy, technology and learning. It is almost as if teaching is widely seen as something that involves just becoming proficient with a few techniques, and that these can be applied to all manner of classroom conditions—including the rapid, mass introduction of new technologies. Initiating learners into good literacy practices, involving new technologies, is a demanding undertaking, and calls for a powerful base of professional knowhow, as well as considerable technical understanding and knowledge of social practices.

The site studies affirm that good practice involves a combination of two qualities: a reflective process, in which teachers subject their pedagogy to theoretically informed scrutiny; and a grounded familiarity with computer technologies. For some teachers, long years of working with computers, with lots of space for experimentation along the way, have brought the kind of fluent performance that Gee (1996) associates with the mode of 'acquisition'. As with becoming a fluent performer in any social practice, there is no real substitute for extended immersion in 'mature' forms of the social practices in which new technologies are embedded (Gee, Hull & Lankshear 1996). This kind of fluent performance is enhanced by knowledge and understandings obtained via the mode of learning, which adds meta-knowledge about the practices. Implementing teachers first means doing the best we can to ensure that teachers have opportunities to both 'acquire' and 'learn' at the interface of literacy and new technologies.

Another aspect of teachers first, evident in the site studies, relates to teachers participating in communities of practice beyond their immediate workplace—for example, as active members of computing clubs or 'listservs'. Through such experiences, teachers undergo continuous professional development, which is fundamental to supporting the teachers-first principle. Teachers with such expertise come to classrooms with the capacity to better 'negotiate' the new communication and information technologies and so influence the organisation of computerised classrooms to meet a variety of educational goals.

In addition, many teachers need more access to computers, and time allocations for preparing and exploring software and hardware resources. In some sites, teachers first was enacted as an integral school practice, giving full recognition to the importance of technical support within classes and in-house professional development programs. It is important that teachers have opportunities to 'rehearse' new technology-mediated activities and projects at least a term before running them. Ignoring the teachers-first principle impedes smooth implementation of new technologies into the school curriculum. It increases dependence on a few enthusiasts, leaving classroom practice vulnerable to fragility.

Finally, supporting teachers first entails school staff development and curricular priorities. However, devoting time to upgrading skills and knowledge in the area of computer hardware and software means less time available for other initiatives, which raises questions about what is valued in the overall school mission.

Complementarity

'Complementarity' emphasises the importance of understanding, in as broad a context as possible, just what is involved in adopting a particular technology. To use a technology effectively is rarely a matter of learning some simple, self-contained, exhaustive skill. Effective use is typically a matter of becoming proficient with a range of interlocking, complementary procedures, knowledges, understandings and dexterities. A good example is learning how to use a calculator. This is not a simple matter of switching the apparatus on and pressing function and number keys. To use a calculator effectively requires at least two complementary skills: ability to estimate an answer, and knowledge of significant figures.

Similarly, complementarity holds for computing technologies—such as using the internet for gathering information and using presentation software. We need to pay attention to the complementary skills and knowledge necessary for sensible, purposeful use of hardware and software. These skills and understandings include knowing about the limits, assumptions and approximations built into hardware and software. Thoughtless use of software is equivalent to blindly assigning it roles that either do not exist or would be better served by other means. Because the internet is such a recent phenomenon, many of the complementary skills and understandings for its effective use are yet to be identified. It seems reasonable, however, to think in terms of teaching and learning aspects of the design and assumptions built into search engines along with the ability to operate them. Similarly, it is important to understand the difference between *obtaining* data on the one hand, and *analysing, organising* and *evaluating* them on the other. Information-gathering tools do precisely that: they gather information. That is the least part of the exercise. Teaching the use of information-gathering tools should occur in association with learning how and when to operate other 'technologies', such as: principles of sound reasoning, how to develop taxonomies, and how to assess the validity and relevance of data. Such an approach goes far beyond simple-minded checklists for 'how to evaluate internet resources'.

Complementarity works at diverse levels. In countries where there are high rates of student use of computers in homes, albeit with unevenly distributed access in demographic terms, complementarity can be applied in relation to home and school. For example, schools could provide access to specialised computer resources that are not available in homes, to build on existing student proficiencies. It is also important that schools apply complementarity in ways that consider students from less advantaged homes with little or no computer access or access to the cultural capital of computing.

As a principle for classroom practice, complementarity speaks to important aspects of the discontinuity, fragility and authenticity patterns. It also honours the three-dimensional nature of literacy as social practice, as operational, cultural and critical capacities are seen as essential to being literate in the information age.

The importance of complementary skills at the literacy–technology interface is evident in teachers' talk about the pressures they experience when they have to acquire new skills and when they have to teach their students new skills. Teachers in the sites voiced a strong sense that they cannot ignore social and cultural demands to familiarise students with new technologies. They regard it as the school's responsibility to prepare students for the world beyond school, and see new technologies as increasingly central to that world. Some speak of the need to prepare students to work in non-linear environments, to learn how to skim, to work in a layered way, to read the visual, to evaluate critically and to select valuable resources from the web. There is a widespread feeling that the literacy skills demanded in using the new technologies represent new literacies that students need for coping in a changing world. These feelings and beliefs, however, tended to outstrip the practices we observed.

In most of the site studies, most of the time, new technologies were employed to gather information for specific classroom assignments and projects. The emphasis on gathering information, at the expense of critically assessing it, highlights the importance of complementarity. It makes apparent the need for explicit engagement of the cultural dimension of technoliteracy practices, with a view to developing skills for critically evaluating as well as collecting information. In most of the sites, students did not engage in exploring the cultural meanings of technoliteracy practices. Nor did these activities emphasise the importance of students adopting critical stances towards information or, more generally, towards the uses of new technologies in everyday social practices. Lack of explicit learning objectives for these critical thinking skills have important implications for school-to-workplace transitions. Many teachers are beginning to see that classrooms need to include a greater emphasis on video editing, animation, graphics and use of the internet. Global objectives include the ability to transfer skills from one medium to another, problem-solving strategies, collaborative work, and an emphasis on divergent thinking.

The lack of attention to the cultural and critical dimensions undoubtedly had a lot to do with the fact that students and teachers alike were closely involved in learning new operations. At the same time, it is important for realising syllabus objectives that the critical and cultural dimensions of literacy be taken into account as far as possible in conjunction with operational learning. This is always likely to be more of a challenge where access to equipment, operational knowledge and prior experience are scarce than it will be under more abundant circumstances. The fact that relatively little critical emphasis was evident during any of the sessions observed across the entire project may indicate the extent to which classroom practices involving new technologies are being exhausted on coming to grips with the operational dimension. The minimal attention given to the critical dimension is understandable, given the relatively limited prior experience many teachers have had with communication and information technologies. It does, however, reinforce the importance of attending to all the patterns and principles identified here in future policy directions at federal, state and school levels, and in professional development and teacher education initiatives.

Workability

'Workability' signals the acid test for implementing any new technology in schools: Does it improve the teaching and learning cycle? And, if there is improvement, is it a better alternative to innovations that could otherwise be considered? To assess workability when introducing new communication and information technologies means taking into account hidden costs, such as those associated with teachers' time in learning how to use them, with redesigning curriculum, and with modifying learning programs. Workability demands that the use of any hardware or software demonstrably improves, helps or supports the work of teachers and students. Workability also needs to affirm that teachers' and students' work is a priority in deciding whether or not to implement a given technology. Adopting new technologies always requires an ethical approach that acknowledges actual costs associated with taking them on.

The workability principle relates directly to issues arising from each of the patterns of practice identified above. It is obvious from what has been said that whether or not introducing a new technology under given conditions will improve the teaching and learning cycle can be determined only by reference to complexity, discontinuity and fragility. The case for conservation and authenticity will become more apparent in our account of the fifth and final principle we present, the 'focus on trajectories'. In brief, school learning is effective to the extent that it is linked appropriately to related social practices in the world beyond school.

While some teachers talk about communication and information technologies as just one more tool that can be used to enhance learning and problem-solving, others see them as springboards for developing innovative ways of teaching reading and writing. Such teachers also see their potential for promoting different ways of investigating new sources of information and for creating new forms of text (Snyder 1996). From this perspective, integrating communication and information technologies into classroom literacy activities contributes to workability by improving the teaching and learning cycle. The reason is that what people need to learn in order to participate in contemporary social, economic and cultural mainstream life increasingly includes new technoliteracy practices. Clearly, taking account of relevant learning needs enhances the teaching and learning cycle. However, practice that is uninformed can easily outweigh the virtue of trying to ensure relevance.

Complex interconnections and interdependencies exist between new technologies and literacy practices (Green 1997a, 1997b; Lankshear 1997; Peters & Lankshear 1996; Snyder 1997). It takes a lot of time to learn how to use multimedia technologies effectively, and then to integrate them into classroom activities and purposes. And teachers see this as a problem, even when they are satisfied with the level of resources and professional development opportunities (for example, Abbotsdale and Ealing Grammar). It is a key factor to be considered with respect to workability.

Not surprisingly, expenditure on hardware and software can be considered a minor part of the workability equation. The real costs of effective use are associated with teachers' time in learning how to operate the technologies, also with teachers' time in gaining the knowledge and understanding required to design and implement classroom learning activities that integrate the technologies in pedagogically sound ways. Effective integration includes providing genuine opportunities for students to acquire relevant cultural and critical understandings, as well as operational knowledge. It also demands that schools ask tough questions. For instance, schools need to decide at what point the benefits of offering students opportunities to work with new technology applications are overshadowed by the risks of apprenticing them to inferior versions of social practices.

Equity

The 'equity' principle affirms that decisions about resource allocation are always involved in using new technologies. Decisions are often made more difficult because new technologies tend to get concentrated in particular curriculum areas, and certainly get concentrated in relation to economic resources. In some cases, decisions to allocate resources to new technologies, as a means of upgrading and re-equipping a school, build on prior knowledge of existing resources. Having some communication and information technologies in the first place, or at least some quality information about them, provides an advantageous base from which to make decisions. Take-up is made difficult where resources and expertise are unevenly distributed—between schools or across curriculum areas in a school. Schools and curriculum areas that are 'resources-poor' in equipment and knowledge end up getting less, while those with some get more—the principle of increasing returns (see Waldrop 1992). It is important to build up sufficient knowledge in disadvantaged areas to enable them to attract material resources by 'natural' means—that is, by making sites that are 'knowledge-poor' less so. Likewise, schools must be able to pursue effective strategies to buffer disadvantaged students from the effects of the uneven distribution of material resources and information. Equity has direct significance for dealing with issues of continuity and fragility. It also bears on issues of authenticity, as 'unauthentic' practice is to a large extent a legacy of being resource- and knowledge-poor.

In the sites, we often saw students assuming powerful roles as experts, who could assist and guide their peers and teachers in using the new technologies. That some learners have greater physical access to tools than others inescapably sets up conditions for unequal opportunities and outcomes—especially when the tools in question are part and parcel of esteemed and rewarded social performances. As formal education is increasingly devolved to local levels, it becomes absolutely essential to establish guarantees that limit physical access disparities as far as possible (Knobel & Lankshear 1997). We found cases where concerted efforts were made to educate everyone fairly in terms of access to learning new technologies. In the Carlisle study, for example, the teacher developed a well-structured timetable to ensure equity of access to resources such as the computer. The result was that, despite the poor computer–student ratio, students saw themselves as having constant access.

At the same time, it is clear that technical proficiency alone accounts for only a proportion of the variation between the ways people mobilise new technologies for literacy purposes. Even if technical training were held constant, literacy practices and activities, drawing on these technical proficiencies, would vary greatly. We have known this for a long time in relation to other learning technologies, but have failed to build the insight into inclusive and democratic educational practices. If anything, the technicist fetish, evident in the most recent language and literacy policies, is taking us in the opposite direction. Many current approaches to remediation, diagnosis, assessment and reporting emphasise and privilege code-breaking and limited aspects of text participation over other essential dimensions of becoming successful readers (Freebody 1992). This creates contexts in which different cultural capitals and funds of knowledge can play out in ways that intensify unequal opportunities for access to social commodities (Gee 1996). For learners in classrooms, the implication is that equity demands not merely attending to matters of physical access to machines and software but also ensuring good learning opportunities to gain proficiency with the cultural and critical aspects of technoliteracy practices that make for socially rewarded forms of competence.

A parallel point holds for teachers as well. Taking account of equity, at the level of distribution of teacher skills and understandings in the area of literacy and new technologies, calls for much more than attending to basic technical skills, although this is important. Familiar calls for 'more professional development and inservicing' are often underinformed, betraying a magical consciousness with respect to the powers of training packages (Freire 1972). Of course, this does not mean holding back on demands for improved professional development opportunities and in-service teacher education. Rather, we need to make informed demands, and to meet these demands with informed responses. This involves widening our focus on the issues surrounding the role of new technologies in education in general and literacy education in particular. Efforts to better prepare ourselves for integrating new technologies into inclusive literacy education must be informed by research explaining the different technoliteracy practices, as well as the different social, economic and cultural rewards associated with their use.

The analysis of the site studies also cautions teachers to be aware of the blurring of boundaries between school and home communication and information technologies access. While such blurring can be exploited by the education community, we need to be aware of the issues of equity and access in a context where the gap between the information-rich and the information-poor is widening. It is important to ensure that students who do not have access to communication and information technologies at home are given adequate access at school, and that opportunities are available out of class time. These students may also require access to instruction that other students familiar with the medium do not need. Greater consideration given to timetabling of facilities may assist in ensuring equitable access.

Rich data for developing viable notions of access and equity in relation to new technology-mediated educational opportunities are provided by the site studies. Access is about much more than the physical availability of infrastructure alone (Burbules 1997; Knobel & Lankshear 1997). To have access to social practices, mediated by new technologies, on equitable terms, has a lot to do with communities of learners being initiated into activities in the presence of genuine familiarity and expertise. Fluent performance can be acquired through immersion in practices with supportive guidance, structuring, explaining and modelling by expert performers.

Focus on trajectories

This principle has to do with the general requirements for learning to be efficacious. It is bound up with the relationship between school and society, and between school forms of learning and social practice in the wider world. When we take a sociocultural approach to learning, our attention shifts, somewhat, from children and schools. From a sociocultural perspective the focus of learning is 'human lives seen as trajectories through multiple social practices and in various social institutions' (Gee, Hull & Lankshear 1996: 4). School learning, conceived in these terms, is not simply for school. It becomes part of a process of initiating children into ways of thinking, acting, believing, valuing and being—Gee's Discourses—that operate beyond the school. As we have noted previously, for learning to be efficacious, what a person does now as a learner 'must be connected in meaningful and motivating ways to "mature" (insider) versions of related social practices' (1996: 4). Learning must be connected to the sorts of things people do at later points in their life trajectories.

The focus on trajectories relates directly to the interface between literacy, technology and learning, and to the patterns of discontinuity, conservation and authenticity. It enlarges our conception of continuity, to take into account 'the long view' of preparing learners for successful participation in forms of social practice that are presumed to be related to school practices. Continuity is not simply a matter of 'scope and sequence at close quarters'—semester to semester, subject area to subject area, one grade to the next—although it certainly includes that. It is also a matter of scope and sequence from school to outside world, from child to adult, from student to worker, from student to citizen. This principle challenges us to have an eye to 'mature' (insider) versions of social practices, and to resist accommodating new technologies to familiar school routines to the extent that this subverts 'authentic' uses of new technologies beyond the school.

In describing this principle, we have emphasised the importance of school learning practices, connecting in meaningful and motivating ways with 'mature' (insider) versions of related social practices, as this is what 'efficacious learning' involves. We have pointed to questionable relationships between school learning practices and related social practices in the world beyond the school. And we have expressed a preference for school learning to contract some kinds of meaningful relationships to outside Discourses. It is important to recognise, however, that the concept of 'efficacious learning', advocated here, does not necessarily require school Discourses to begin initiating children into 'mature' versions of outside social practices. The 'trajectory' principle can be met by children's school-based learning now, connecting in meaningful and motivating ways to their school-based learning later. This is a coherent and possibly viable option, especially in relation to literacy education and new technologies. If classroom learning now need only prepare learners for distinctively school-like literacy practices involving new technologies later, then we can probably accept a trajectory that runs from 'digitised children's literature' activities to 'writing stories for school newspapers'. We need to question the point of school-based Discourses in general as well as of specific school-based Discourses such as literacy education (Gee, Hull & Lankshear 1996). Current initiatives to integrate new technologies into classroom literacy education provide us with a new context and incentive for revisiting this crucial issue.

If, however, we decide that school-based learning is 'authentic', in terms of social practices in the world beyond the school, it is vital that education not be reduced merely to socialising learners into established social practices. This would fly in the face of the critical dimension of education overall, and of literacy and technology education in particular. Hence, while 'authentic' learning might be preferred over narrow initiation into school Discourse, the educational end has to be more than successful indoctrination into selected status-quo practices. The right to education implies the right to be prepared for democratic life as an active citizen, who can and will contribute to transforming social practices where they need to be transformed.

The patterns and principles outlined in this chapter provide a useful framework for understanding the educational concerns surrounding the integration of new technologies into classroom-based learning. The framework is also useful for making sense of how school practices can be enabled or impeded in attempts to promote desired learning outcomes. In chapter 6, we draw on this framework, as well as on key ideas introduced in earlier chapters, to offer some practical suggestions for pursuing developments in curriculum and pedagogy in schools and education systems.

6 Practical suggestions for future developments

A WHOLE-SCHOOL, HIGH-COMMITMENT RESPONSE

School teachers and administrators are currently subjected to a range of forces which push teaching in the direction of a formulaic, mechanistic, 'painting by numbers' engagement, and which seek to remake teachers, particularly at primary-school level, into technicians. The role of such 'technician-teachers' would increasingly be to implement packaged programs sold on the promise of offering the best method or 'fix' in town. This trend is especially apparent in literacy education, where commercial developers, freelancers and university 'researcher-consultants' fight it out for the chance to 'deliver' off-the-shelf, packaged approaches to literacy, remedial intervention programs, diagnostic kits, together with training in their use. Such initiatives reduce literacy and learning to the operational dimension, and represent the latest chapter in the quest—beloved of many policy-makers, politicians and top-level 'educrats'—for a 'teacher-proof' curriculum. Yet they are often welcomed, seen as credible in the context of a one-dimensional literacy plan, that will provide the basis for an intensified regimen of testing and escalating reporting requirements.

The combination of growing administrative demands on teachers' time, larger classes with more diverse student populations, and policy-based reductions of social practices like literacy to operational

132

performances, often called 'competencies', encourages hopes for—even expectations of—ready, sure-fire solutions. And if ever there were a context in which such hopes and expectations seemed warranted, it would surely have to be in the contemporary school context, where great pressure is put on teachers often underprepared for the task to integrate new technologies into classroom learning. Not surprisingly, we cannot go along with this. Educated people are more than merely 'operational'—although they certainly are proficient in the operational dimensions of social practices. More importantly, they understand social practices in 3D. Indeed, capable performance at the operational level, without strong 'insider' cultural knowledge of practices and without the innovator's critical orientation, is a safe passport to marginal status within communities of practice and, often, to low-level employment and constrained life chances.

There is a clear and important message here for teachers. The more teaching gets made into a form of 'routine production work' (Reich 1992), pitched at turning out learners who achieve operational capacity as 'the bottom line', with the assistance of standardised production and measurement techniques, from commercially produced methods and kits to hard-sell software, the more merely operational and deskilled the occupation becomes. Consequently, the more marginal it will become in terms of economic and social status, and the more readily teachers can be displaced by 'para-educators' and machines (Robertson 1998). This is an old message but one that still needs to be heard, including, lamentably, among those who inhabit the corridors of teacher education faculties and universities.

The sociocultural perspective we present in this book affirms that educational work is high-level work, not amenable to easy solutions and quick fixes, electronic or otherwise. From a sociocultural perspective, educational work demands a balance between sound theoretical understanding and high-quality practice. This holds especially for the literacy–technology challenge. It is not a challenge for which teachers can be prepared by means of a clutch of formulaic, off-the-shelf 'gadgets' or quick-fix training and professional development packages. On the contrary, we are convinced that enhanced practice at the literacy–technology–learning interface calls for a good deal of reflective, interpretive thinking work, together with a strong foundation of personal experience of social practices involving new technologies. While some of this work can be done by individuals on their own initiative, it is important that a lot of it be undertaken collectively and collaboratively in the process of building a culture at the whole-school level, as well as in smaller groups and partnerships, based on shared interests and other sources of affiliation.

Working together

Our first practical suggestion for schools committed to enhancing classroom practice at the literacy–technology–learning interface is thus to initiate regular all-staff activities, which analyse the school's current situation rigorously using the concepts, patterns of practice and principles for practice we have developed in previous chapters. The activities could be seen as a form of purposeful, school-based, self-directed professional development, articulated with school-based policy, planning and program development. Although such professional development will be demanding and represents a considerable investment by staff, anything less would be at best a partial response to the challenge.

A program of one to two hours fortnightly would be scheduled, with staff attendance formally required, paid attendance by teacher aides encouraged, and all staff responsible for leading at least one session. At each session, one or two staff members would briefly introduce and explain a key concept (for example, the 3D model of social practices), a pattern of practice (for example, fragility or conservation) or a principle for practice (for example, complementarity, teachers first). For the remainder of each session participants, collectively or in groups, depending on staff size, would discuss, interpret and assess the significance of the particular concept, pattern or principle in the context of their school and individual classrooms. They would also brainstorm a range of possible responses to the concept, pattern or principle's implications for practice in their own setting. They would then rank the possible responses according to importance, selecting priorities for inclusion in the school plan and specific policies such as literacy, technology and resourcing. By the time most or all of the concepts, patterns and principles have been tackled in this way—which might take a semester to achieve—a number of overlaps, links and groups of ideas will have emerged. These will help to identify orders of priority and potential approaches to be pursued in strategic planning, needs analysis and team-building.

Getting advice

Depending on a school's resources and contacts, it could seek paid or voluntary participation from outside personnel with relevant kinds of expertise. These people could include parents of students, connections in the school community area, state education department personnel, retailers, academics and researchers. Relevant expertise could range from troubleshooting skills, group facilitation and team-building capabilities, technical knowledge relating to resourcing options, policy development capacities, scenario-building experience, and familiarity with related social practices involving new technologies.

While this kind of activity and commitment is taxing on resources of energy, time and goodwill, it can be powerfully educative—particularly when it is well-planned, well-managed, and when tasks are equitably distributed. For example, the job of identifying relevant outside expertise becomes a process of finding out just what is relevant expertise and where this resides. It involves more than simply thinking of the first likely candidate. Rather, it entails developing some theories about social practices and what it means to be expert in them, doing some grassroots research about who is expert in what, following up leads and taking advice. While this kind of work requires time and effort, it may well yield more lasting and deeper educational consequences than other equally challenging options, such as doing a degree or diploma course, organising fund-raising to meet budget shortfalls, and otherwise 'running around in circles'.

This type of 'big commitment' initiative will work only if there is strong leadership from the principal, senior administrators, subject heads (in the case of secondary schools), and members of staff who have authority and respect. On any staff, of any size, there is likely to be a mix of more and less enthusiastic participants—including those who are very reluctant. Unless leaders are seen as fully committed to the exercise, supporting it strongly, it is unreasonable to expect such initiatives to succeed as a culture-building and a culture-changing endeavour. By the same token, if a school is serious about meeting challenges imposed by important changes in social practices and conditions which affect teaching and learning, this is precisely the kind of authoritative leadership and collegial commitment necessary.

For our part, as authors and researchers, we have aimed to describe, ground and explain our key concepts, patterns and principles as clearly as we can to maximise their potential as an organising framework for school-based policy, curriculum and professional development. In the end, however, we cannot possibly reformulate these ideas into precise practical applications and strategies for the very different kinds of schools and conditions that exist. As with all concepts, the potential contribution of those we have advanced here depends on the quality and extent of their uptake by committed professionals, who are prepared to relate them thoughtfully to their own environments and practices. Here, as elsewhere in education, 'one size does not fit all'.

CONTRACT WITH THE READER

Nonetheless, the research, theorising and experiences that inform this book allow us to advance some more or less concrete and specific suggestions in addition to the initiative we have just described. Moreover, writers of books like this one have a tacit 'contract' with their readers to do the best they can to facilitate productive uptake and practical applications of the ideas and judgments put forward. Below we describe four sets of strategies, activities and applications that emerge from what we have said.

Pedagogical pointers

Here we describe three procedures designed to enhance teaching and learning in the area of literacy and new technologies.

Think social practice in 3D

Effective learning builds on understanding the rationale of what is being learned and how it fits into a larger scheme of human activities and purposes. Because the sense that we as teachers make of learning activities and purposes differs from the sense students make of them, we most often depend on luck and coincidence for planned learning to occur. A large research literature now exists, much of it concerned with literacy, which documents the relationship between learning failure, or low levels of learning attainment, and students either not understanding the point of what is going on or having a different understanding from the teachers and successful students (Boomer 1988; Bourdieu 1977; Delgado-Gaitan 1990; Delpit 1995; Heath 1983; Jones 1986; Michaels 1986; Moll 1992).

Other than when it is a senseless activity, which unfortunately it sometimes is, learning is a process of entry into and participation in some Discourse or other: that is, some social practice where people, words, beliefs, actions, tools, artefacts, values, standards, goals and purposes get integrated in meaningful ways, and where we come to see what is involved in playing a particular role and performing it proficiently (Gee 1996, 1997; Gee, Hull & Lankshear 1996). Obvious as this might be, it is sobering to reflect on the extent to which students fail to learn in classrooms because they misconceive or otherwise cannot grasp the social practice they are supposed to be getting initiated into.

Often when learners fail to grasp the point of what is going on in the classroom, it is because the practice does not mesh well with their other experiences. This is often a matter of cultural mismatching (Heath 1982, 1983). It may occur, however, because there is no obviously intelligible practice going on—as when skills are 'taught' in decontextualised ways. A good example, from the area of literacy and new technologies, concerned a class learning to use email through the medium of a game that involved students from several schools sending and receiving cryptic clue messages in an attempt to track down a fictitious criminal. The activity continued for several weeks, at the end of which the Year 7 student who was the subject of the study told the researcher it had been fun, but she did not really know what it was all about. There was certainly a social practice going on, but it was an odd and obfuscating one for anyone, like the student in question, coming at it cold. Is this what emailing involves? Is emailing about game playing? What is the learning focus here? Do these technical operations—logging on, checking the in-box—belong to the game (Knobel 1999)?

Slogans like 'make it explicit' have emerged in recognition that classroom practice is often obfuscating. A good rule of thumb for all teaching is to clarify to ourselves, as teachers, just what social practice the class is going to be involved in. If we are not clear about that, it is unlikely that learners will be. Moreover, it is only once we have an unambiguous idea of what the social practice is going to be that we can reflect on the likely points of connection and disconnection for different groups of learners, and whether what we are doing and the way we are doing it is optimal in terms of learner trajectories. Being able to name the social practice that given learning activities belong to is a precondition for being able to make learning explicit and for finding ways of making it accessible to learners with different cultural backgrounds and learning histories. Very often we think we have made something explicit when we have spoken about it. But that is not enough if learners are unable to see the learning in relation to practices they can get a handle on (Gee 1996; Gee, Hull & Lankshear 1996).

Getting clear about the underlying social practice is especially important in areas of learning where teachers lack strong knowledge and experience, as is often the case when communication and information technologies are used. Young people who have grown up with new technologies may become thoroughly confused, or bored and disaffected, when confronted with 'odd' or 'naive' practices introduced by teachers in desperate attempts to find uses for new technologies. To promote effective learning, we need to be clear that we are involving learners in a coherent social practice with which they can make some genuine connections. The closer we stick to 'authentic' forms of social practice and to 'mature' versions of these, the safer we are likely to be.

The clearer we are about the social practice involved, the better our chances of enabling learners to grasp and become proficient at the operational, cultural and critical dimensions of the literacy associated with it. The more familiar we are with a social practice, the easier it is to identify its operational, social and cultural dimensions and to create and scaffold learning activities. Equally, the more familiar we are with alternative versions of that practice, the easier it is to identify its critical dimension and to generate effective learning activities.

The key point here is that teachers are provided with curriculum requirements to meet, but are left with the task of working out how to structure suitable learning activities. Where learning fails, it is often for want of learners seeing the meaningfulness of the larger practice. The more transparently we can embed specific learning tasks in meaningful social practices, the more likely it is that learners will grasp not only the operational aspects but the important cultural and critical dimensions as well (Heath & McLaughlin 1994; Heath & Mangiola 1991).

Begin with the cultural

Teaching and learning are always situated in unique contexts and always situate their participants in unique ways, producing distinctive 'local' learning effects. Even so, we can advance some ideas here about how to integrate the 3D approach into school-based learning. We suggest to begin by prioritising the cultural dimension: to emphasise 'authentic' meaning-making and appropriate action within a given community of practice (Durrant & Green 1998). As we have maintained throughout our discussion, classroom learning is ideally linked to, and in the service of, 'real-life' and lifelike social practices. Effective learning involves making schools and classrooms as much as possible into 'worldly', socially meaningful places, characterised

by what Jo-Anne Reid (1997: 150) describes as 'generic practice'—
'the engaged production of social texts for real purposes'.

Whatever the lesson or unit of work, and at whatever level of
schooling, the task is to find ways of encouraging and helping
learners to become participants in particular communities of social
practice, so that they can learn to become 'insiders' in that practice
—that is, proficient members of the group(s) who engage in that
practice. The task represents a process of recruiting and initiating
learners into Discourses in school settings, in ways that parallel how
people get recruited and initiated into communities of practice in
all sorts of other institutions, such as families, clubs and churches.

The ideals of generic practice towards which schools should
aspire can be understood in terms of three related ideas. First, while
schools should help prepare learners for participation in social
practices and institutions in the world beyond their walls, they
will not be able to do this in exact, continuous ways because they
are distinctive as institutions. Schools cannot prepare learners for
seamless entry into the practices of other institutions, such as
workplaces and civic organisations, precisely because they are not
those institutions: they are different.

Second, despite these differences, there are generic links
between what schools can and should teach and the practices in
which institutions beyond the school engage. These generic links
include qualities such as the capacity for clear thinking, a sense of
logic, sensitivity to standards, and procedures for 'getting it right'—
whatever 'it' might be. They also include more tangible capacities
that are employed in institutional practices outside school, such
as being able to write clear and grammatically correct sentences,
knowing how to gather relevant information and manipulate it, how
to organise ideas, assess evidence, calculate accurately, control variables, and design experiments.

Third, the sorts of capabilities learned in school, especially
secondary school, should reflect or resemble the distinctively
academic and scholarly practices that exist beyond the school. These
practices include being an historian, a geographer, a literary critic,
a mathematician, an economist and an accountant.

In light of these ideas, school-based learning should aim to keep
the links as close as possible between generic practice and 'real-
world' applications; it should exemplify as far as possible the qualities
of 'mature' academic and scholarly practice. Although enabling learners to become insiders in the culture of the Science or History
classroom will not be exactly the same as enabling them to become

'insiders' in the culture of the research science laboratory of a large company, or to become insiders in the culture of a history project in a university, a government think-tank, or a private consultancy, the fit should be as close as possible. Further, the values, purposes and behaviour of the 'mature' practice should be as 'present' as possible in the school practices from the earliest stages of involvement. Ideally, the same will hold between subject-based learning in Technology, Domestic Science and Manual Arts classrooms and the related outside social practices. Moreover, the generic skills of clear thinking, logical rigour and clarity, and a critical notion of design as learned in school, should carry over readily to applications in the wider world.

What does this mean in practical, pedagogical terms? It means, for example, that if primary-school students are to use new technologies for obtaining information in doing projects or producing reports, this should be approached as an initiation into forms of practice where the emphasis is on knowing: how to access reliable, relevant information efficiently and elegantly; how to ask good questions and what makes the questions good; and when to use internet sources or email in preference to more conventional sources, and why.

These ideas, however, are at odds with increasingly familiar practices, such as having students email students in other countries to 'ask for information'. Whether or not the students in other countries are appropriate sources of good-quality information is debatable. Further, the enthusiasm for using email and making distant contacts may displace the more important learning, which has to do with the construction of knowledge. Moreover, it is doubtful that 'netiquette' is observed in asking a person to provide information in an email message if the information could be obtained readily from another source—not to mention the research principle of obtaining information as efficiently and elegantly as possible.

Equally relevant is the question: What kinds of social practices are students initiated into when they produce 'projects' and 'reports'? This question has been germane for decades—as much in the time of using pencils as now in the time of using computers. To the extent that 'doing projects' and 'producing reports' are about introducing students to participation in social practices which have 'mature' versions in the outside world, the classroom activities should be introducing learners to practices of researching. In this instance, the 'mature' versions of the related social practices are undertaking research projects and writing research reports. The related community of practice is that of researchers. From the outset, research is what the classroom activities should be pointing towards and should determine where the emphasis is placed in learning. Learning to obtain information should focus on the research traits of the activity over the use of email and other 'gadgets'. And if students are to learn to use email in the context of information-gathering activities, they should be acquainted from the outset with the conditions under which it is the suitable technology to use.

Of course, using email to elicit expert opinion does occur within 'mature' communities of research practice. But it is rarely a major source of data, and even more rarely the centrepiece of data collection. The object of classroom learning at the literacy–technology interface, in activities such as projects and writing reports, should be to introduce students in ways appropriate to their levels to bona fide research procedures and habits. This means of course that teachers need to be well informed about research as practice. Unless they are, it is difficult to conceive a sequence of 'research-related learnings' appropriate to various age or grade levels, and to translate these into activities involving particular literacy skills and understandings and fitting uses of new technologies. To emphasise use of technologies without adequate attention to foregrounding the structure and point of the practice is likely to confuse students in the short run and to be counterproductive in the long run, as it sets them on a false trajectory.

Yet when such work is done well it can be impressive, and it is surprising what students can learn. Some of the examples provided by Shirley Brice Heath (1983) in *Ways with Words* still strike us as outstanding: for instance, young learners seeing the difference between the 'shape' of typed transcriptions of their oral language narratives, which they had tape-recorded themselves, and the 'shape' of formal written presentations of the genre they were supposed to be learning. From this basis they were able to understand some crucial aspects of school literacy practices. Such an example presents a remarkable illustration of a sound sense of research being translated into classroom learning.

Similar points hold for other genres, such as biography. As 'insider' practice, producing biographies involves extensive interpretation of lives, not merely piecing chunks of information together around a generic formula, adding illustrations, and producing them as graphically illustrated hard copy or in electronic forms. To prioritise the cultural dimension of practice, and to make it the basis for undertaking operational and critical forms of learning, means starting from a well-grounded understanding of biography as a social practice and of being a biographer as a social identity. If interpretation is fundamental to biography it needs to be foregrounded, and opportunities structured into the learning that call for learners to interpret. Learners should also be introduced to the relationship of the genre—that is, the literacy—to the larger practice of biography, by means of careful scaffolding and direct teaching.

Teachers who have an understanding of biography as social practice and its characteristic forms of embedded literacy—from data collection, including interviewing, to manipulating text for interpretation, to writing up the biography—can construct a coherent sequence of activities for teaching the genre. All sorts of relevant applications of new and old technologies can be used in these activities. Their use, however, might not involve an emphasis on graphics and fonts.

The general point is equally valid at secondary-school levels, where learners are involved in becoming proficient at 'subject-specific literacies' (Green 1988), including embedded uses of new technologies. What does it mean to become an 'insider' in the Economics or History classroom (Durrant & Green 1998)? The answer here depends on how we view the relationship between school Economics or History and related outside Discourses—and which outside Discourses? We could argue, for example, that subjects like Economics and History are useful for the outside Discourses of being a citizen, being an informed consumer, making judgments about events reported in the media, and being an informed traveller—that is to say, outside Discourses of a non-academic or scholarly nature. On the other hand, 'Economics' and 'History' refer to specific social practices and communities of practice, those of economists and historians.

This distinction bears on our understanding of 'historical literacy' and 'economics literacy', as well as on what it means to be an 'insider' in the Economics or History classroom. If Economics and History are seen as concerned with learning bodies of content, comparing and contrasting different viewpoints contained in textbooks, then becoming proficient in the literacy requirements of the subjects, being an insider, amounts to knowing how to write 'good essays' on the basis of information gathered from a range of secondary information sources. Being an insider in the culture of the classroom will mean little more than doing the required reading, answering questions, asking questions (perhaps), referencing sources, indenting quotations, and acquiring skill in essayist writing, as defined by the teacher.

If, however, we take 'being an economist' and 'being a historian' as markers of the 'mature' versions of related social practices, the literacy culture of the classrooms will be very different. History students might be hunting down original archive material and artefacts, integrating them, considering different approaches to historiography, and employing techniques of historical interpretation and data analysis. Economics students might be working with models and simulations, becoming acquainted with a range of competing economic theories, and working with primary data.

The implications for using new technologies in these subjects vary with how we conceive the goals and purposes of teaching and learning, how far we see learning as being about content and how far we see it as also being about early initiation into the craft and tools of the fully fledged historian and economist. If we take the 'becoming proficient with the content and writing good essays' view, computers may be useful for archiving quotations, storing summaries of textbook passages, compiling bibliographies and producing the final essay. The more that 'mature' versions of being an economist or historian are taken as the model for classroom learning, however, the more diverse the classroom applications of new technologies might become. For example, copies of original documents could be scanned into computers for analysis; recorded oral history interviews could be loaded onto the computer using voice-recognition software to provide transcriptions for coding, analysing and cross-referencing. Such procedures do not pertain merely to managing operational aspects of new technologies. They point to key features of the subject literacies and practices of the historian and economist. Reading and writing in the manner of the historian or economist involves very different kinds of texts and ways of obtaining and operating on texts from approaches to learning history that are based on the textbook.

It is not our purpose to pronounce on what 'the proper classroom approach' should be—rather, to say that the literacy–technology interface varies dramatically with different answers to the questions: What is the cultural dimension of History (or Economics, or Maths, or Geography, or Physics) as a social practice? and: What is the cultural dimension of historical literacy (reading and writing, and information-gathering and processing in the manner of a historian)? Our purpose is also to suggest that as teachers we need answers to these questions about the nature of the social practices in which we are engaging students, if we are to promote effective learning within the operational and critical dimensions of these subject-practices. As Durrant and Green (1998: 11) remind us, the value for teachers as a profession of the sociocultural approach to teaching and learning is first that:

> it puts education firmly up front, and that means emphasising literacy and curriculum issues in the classroom and in one's teaching, rather than technology or technical issues. In such a view, the latter are always secondary, or *supplementary*, although importantly never neutral. Technologies *support* learning and teaching, which always remains the main game, and indeed the point of the whole exercise. Hence it is teachers' *educational* expertise that needs to be foregrounded and strengthened, along with their professional knowledge, skills and dispositions, which they then bring to bear on the challenge of the new technologies for schooling and for education more generally. Among other things, this restores the role and the significance of good teaching, and of the teacher as 'expert' in his or her own classroom, charged with drawing children into the culture of learning.
>
> Integrating Information Technology into the Key Learning Areas always, and of necessity, involves drawing on the specific subject-area expertise of teachers. Similarly, constructing coherent, informed, effective literacy programs requires that teachers' professional judgment and their own theories of literacy *and* pedagogy become crucial, first-order resources for curriculum and professional development. Policy-wise, it follows that strategic alliances need to be forged, within schools, between different but related communities of interest and expertise, and new opportunities generated for across-the-curriculum professional dialogue.

Take careful note of the operational and the critical

Prioritising the cultural dimension of social practice, being clear about which social practice we are engaging in, and having a sound understanding of 'mature' forms of related social practices in the world beyond the classroom, make the task of dealing with the operational and critical dimensions of literacy easier to handle: easier from the standpoint of both teachers and learners.

For teachers, especially those who have limited experience and confidence with new technologies, the challenge is often to know on which operational skills and understandings to focus. The sociocultural view of learning provides clear directions here. The benchmark will always be provided by the social practice in its 'mature' form: How do the experts do it? What new technological applications, if any, do they use? Which of these can be employed and taught? and: How can these be taught, given the level of the class and the particular aspects of the practice in which they will be involved?

We need to remember that the operational dimension of a social practice and its associated literacy and technology components may not involve a heavy emphasis on new communication and information technologies. We also need to remember that a person can be a whiz with operational aspects of new technologies without being especially proficient in the practice as a whole. The pedagogical imperative is to get the emphasis in the right place. If the curriculum requirement is to teach the information report genre, there may well be space for introducing operational skills like compiling a table or chart, inserting a diagram, or scanning in a ready-made graph. The prior demand, however, is that these be relevant, reliable and rigorously produced portrayals of information, and that the ways of determining whether this is so are understood. The practice is the dog; the technology is the tail; and the dog should wag the tail. Indeed, if we think of the classroom ʾas a complex, self-organising system, with roles among components to be negotiated at the point where new technology input is required, the chances are better that learners will be able to work out the dog–tail conundrum for themselves.

As far as learners are concerned, the more apparent the nature and demands of the social practice, and the more significant the practice is seen to be, the more readily students will recognise the meaningfulness and relevance of skill development. It becomes clear that having appropriate skills and understandings is imperative to function effectively within a particular Discourse (Durrant & Green 1998). It follows that students will be recruited to learning skills more readily if the curriculum requirements are couched in practice contexts that learners relate to and value. Failure to understand the point of a skill, process or understanding in relation to meaningful practice is a major impediment to effective participation and learning in school. Once again, the teacher's professional ability is challenged to identify appropriate social practices within which to teach specific curriculum requirements and to find ways to map these onto the experiences, understandings and Discourse backgrounds of the students in a class (Gee 1991; Heath 1983; Heath & McLaughlin 1994; Moll 1992).

The critical dimension can be seen as having both internal and external aspects in relation to social practices and their literacies. For example, if students are involved in investigating something about the environment to produce a report, opportunities must be created for them to make critical readings of texts included in their information base, and to make critically informed assessments of the varying perspectives and interests that shape and inform the different texts they are using. These may be conventional print texts or electronic text resources. Such an approach can be seen as critique, which is internal to the social practice of reporting the findings of a text-based investigation. Students are required to make a judgment about where the balance of evidence lies and which views or stances seem most defensible.

However, part of learning what is involved in investigating aspects of the environment, or health, housing and traffic flows, is coming to see that investigations and their reports are always undertaken from some standpoint or other—as, of course, are the texts that make up the information base. Therefore, if students are producing reports, they must understand how to adopt a position from which to undertake their work, or they must understand how to recognise the position they take up. Who are they, or the authors of informing texts, in this practice? A newspaper reporter looking to make a splash? A parent with concerns about chemical waste dumping in the area? A Green Peace worker? A researcher hired by a strip-mining company? Being able to identify the point of view marks the external component of the critical dimension, where the focus of critique is the practice itself, defined in relation to the position from which it is taken up.

Becoming an informed, effective 'insider' of a social practice is one thing, albeit important: after all, if one is going to participate in a community of practice, the ideal is to be an effective, informed and proficient performer of that practice. However, having a critical perspective on that social practice, as a participant in it, is a different order of things altogether. One might be a very competent environmental writer for strip-mining companies and toxic waste dumpers with the ability to 'win the day' for their interests. But ought one want to be? A critical perspective suggests asking reflexive questions such as: How might one practise this role with maximum integrity? It provokes questions about the culture and the community and about whom one is expected to be and become (Durrant & Green 1998).

As learning is about entry into and participation in some social practice or other that helps shape who and what we are, do, think, value, believe and aspire to, it is incumbent on teachers to ensure that learners have opportunities both to become competent in socially recognised and rewarded practices and their embedded literacies and to know how to transform these practices from within as they deem appropriate, or how and when to 'leave' them in preference for others. The capacity to foster this kind of learning rests squarely on teachers' understandings of social practices and of the different perspectives (strip-mine advocate, 'Green', or concerned parent) from which these practices can be engaged.

Strategies for developing policies, plans and programs

Plan before purchasing
In 1998 a group of leading-edge, North American commentators on the cultural evolution of new technologies in social practices drafted eight principles of 'technorealism', signed the document, then launched it as a charter. They aimed to intervene in a situation where 'despite the complicated and often contradictory implications of technology, the conventional wisdom is woefully simplistic' (Shenk 1998: 217). Polarised thinking—in the form of 'breathless tales of either high-tech doom or cyber-elation'—can result only in 'dashed hopes and unnecessary anxiety, and [prevent] us from understanding our own culture' (1998: 217). Among the principles of technorealism are several that mesh tightly with the positions we are advancing in this book. For example: 'Technologies are not neutral'; 'The Internet is revolutionary, but not Utopian'; 'Government has an important role to play on the electronic frontier'; 'Information is not knowledge'; 'Understanding technology is an essential component of global citizenship'. Most significantly, for our immediate purposes, the fifth principle of technorealism states: 'Wiring the schools will not save them'. The authors elaborate as follows (1998: 218):

> The problems with America's public schools . . . have almost
> nothing to do with technology. Consequently, no amount of
> technology will lead to the educational revolution prophesied by
> President Clinton and others. The art of teaching cannot be
> replicated by computers, the Net, or by 'distance learning'. These
> tools can, of course, augment an already high quality educational
> experience. But to rely on them as any sort of educational panacea
> would be a costly mistake.

While a lot more work remains to be done on the subject, one well-respected estimate of a high-quality, technology-rich education says that only somewhere between 20 and 30 per cent of the costs have to do with hardware and software (Becker 1996). Becker's work is based on US secondary schools, where he reasons that costs run at about US$2000 per student per year, of which about 25 per cent involves hardware and software. This figure is probably conservative when, for example, we recognise the amount of time, which equals money, required for something as elementary as learning how to use a word-processing program or a new version of one.

Our earlier account of the 'three pedagogical pointers' helps explain such calculations. The kind of 'high-quality educational experiences' that can be 'augmented' by 'computers, the Net and "distance learning"' draw heavily on deep professional knowledge and experience (Shenk 1998: 218). This knowledge includes being able to arrive at cogent answers to questions about the relationship between school Discourses and outside Discourses, and about how to honour the principle of efficacious learning, which requires that what is learned now relates in meaningful and motivating ways to what people do later. The task of translating policy and syllabus requirements into learning activities grounded in meaningful, social practices that relate to later trajectory points through social institutions and practices is demanding. Yet it underpins a high-quality education, and has to be present for the integration of new technologies into effective learning activities.

If schools are to integrate new technologies into high-quality educational learning experiences, they need to do their sums and organise the purchasing of equipment around clear, informed and careful planning. As far as possible, schools need to ensure that teachers know more than how to drive the machines. To enable them to respond in sound, pedagogical ways to the various patterns and principles identified in chapter 5, teachers need to know about the interdependence between the operational, cultural and critical dimensions of classroom technoliteracy practices.

Adopt whole-school, cross-curriculum, integrated approaches to policy and planning
The best response to patterns of fragility and discontinuity, that honours principles such as complementarity, workability and equity, is to ensure that school plans, programs and policies are developed on a whole-school, cross-curriculum basis.

Durrant and Green (1998) argue that in today's world, perhaps

more than ever before, the socially recognised and rewarded understandings are communication and information skills of the
'symbolic-analytic' variety (see also Reich 1992). These are not just
skills like spelling and keyboarding, but include those associated
with design, critical analysis, and electronic forms of information
access and handling (Durrant & Green 1998).

To help provide a sound initiation into such skills and understandings, schools need to work from an informed sense of the
nature and scope of information and communications tools, applications and processes. Curriculum needs to ensure that an
appropriate range and balance of information and communication
applications and procedures are taken into account. Curriculum also
needs to integrate distinctively new technological elements, for
example using search engines with more established and familiar
aspects, such as logical analysis and critical appraisal. The two kinds
of resources below are particularly helpful for teachers tackling these
tasks.

Exemplars of integrated, whole-school policy development and planning. Some
excellent exemplars exist of whole-school, cross-curriculum planning.
For example, at Abbotsdale, Robert the teacher had collaborated with
a teacher-librarian from a neighbouring school and the region's
learning technology officer to frame a sequence of computing skills
and concepts designed to cover Years 1 to 7, and to optimise the
school's finite new-technology resources. Their plan became the
school's technology policy. As he had also been a key participant
in developing the school's language policy, Robert could work with
his colleagues on the technology policy to sequence the introduction
of specific computing concepts and skills in accordance with learning activities in language and, indeed, across the curriculum learning
areas. The curriculum plan built on the premise that all computing
skills are at the same time concepts: you do not teach and learn only
a skill but also the associated concept.

Concept-skills were identified under six category headings: word-
processing, desktop publishing, spreadsheet, database, drawing/
painting and communications. Coverage was comprehensive,
with more than 40 concept-skills identified for word-processing
alone. Once introduced, the various concept-skills were included in
learning activities for all subsequent years—to maintain fluency in
their use and to build a comprehensive integration. At the same
time, sequencing was matched as closely as possible to teacher
knowledge and experience, as well as to machines. As a result, online

communications concepts and skills were built in from Year 5 through Year 7, where teacher expertise existed. Moreover, Abbotsdale, which was an economically disadvantaged school, did not have to provide internet connections and technical support for every classroom. Teachers and schools that produce such plans and policies are typically happy to share them with others. Schools with less experience and confidence can easily obtain access to such exemplars by asking for them from department officers, professional associations or through listservs.

Conceptual tools. Informing the kind of approach taken at Abbotsdale are conceptual tools, such as classifications, and categories, which 'map' the scope of technoliteracy practices and help with planning for scope, sequence and comprehensive coverage. Abbotsdale's classification of word-processing, desktop publishing, spreadsheet, database, drawing/painting and communications is one such conceptual tool. A similar kind of conceptual tool is the literacy/computing classification scheme we advanced in chapter 2.

The development of conceptual tools involves the process of thinking about the range of new technological applications in relation to literacy practices. The tools are generated to support further reflection, interpretation, and 'translation' within activities like whole-school planning and programming across the curriculum. By using such tools, identifying their strengths and limitations in relation to our own needs, purposes and circumstances, and building on insight obtained through grounded professional development, we learn to produce our own refined 'models'. On reaching that point of independence, it is likely that classroom programs will have taken a great leap forward in educational terms. Such is the relationship between reflection and practice. Such also are the results of operating as a reflective practitioner. The bottom line is that there are simply no quick fixes or easy solutions: only committed and challenging reflective-practical-theoretical work of the kind that makes classrooms into truly 'educational' spaces.

Of course, conceptual tools can be applied in an informed and systematic manner only if curriculum development, planning and programming, and the policy practices that guide them and to which they are accountable, are undertaken on a whole-school, cross-curriculum basis. Otherwise, gaps and redundancies will occur, and both human and infrastructural resources will be unevenly distributed and deployed.

The challenge for schools is to provide a comprehensive, integrated approach to professional development at the interface of literacy, technology and learning, in principled, informed and educationally effective ways. Our ideals of 'across-the-curriculum, collaborative, whole-school efforts to build a learning culture with links to the community' should be useful in meeting this challenge. At the most overt and tangible level, it involves mapping technological and conventional literacies to subject areas on a topic-by-topic, subject-by-subject, semester-by-semester, year-by-year basis. This process will help identify areas where individuals and teams need to focus their professional development work as well as priorities for resourcing, staffing, recruitment and departmental support.

Recruit strategically
One benefit of a holistic approach to curriculum programming, policy planning and professional development is that it makes it easier for a school to approach its staffing needs strategically. As positions are vacated or created, schools can proactively recruit new staff with an eye to the sorts of detailed specialisms, as well as more general strengths and experiences, required to maximise their literacy–technology effort.

Lobby proactively and disseminate information
Schools are not the only educational organisations that have been caught short in the literacy–technology challenge. Teacher education institutions and education departments are in the same boat. Given the lead time involved in training teachers, the sooner teacher education institutions become informed about what kinds of teachers are needed in classrooms, the more quickly schools will adapt to current and future demands. While comprehensive, school-based, professional development initiatives along the lines we have described can take up some of the slack, teacher education institutions need strong and informed guidance as to how to make their programs at the literacy–technology interface more appropriate. Schools that have engaged in integrated, intensive planning and programming will be in a strong position to lobby for change in teacher education. There is considerable evidence at present that such change is needed.

In addition, schools that make progress along the lines we are advocating will be well placed to illuminate education department policies. At present, many departmental policies do little more than emphasise operational competencies—for teachers and learners alike. Moreover, they often harness teacher competencies with new technologies to outmoded routines that bypass the kinds of thinking by teachers called for by a sociocultural approach to literacy, technology and learning. Lists of static technology competencies for teachers that are tied to requirements like producing worksheets, assessing student-learning activities, and using at least one or two curriculum and one or two generic software packages, fall far short of what policy guidelines for teachers and teacher educators need to incorporate. Schools can play important roles in moving policy forward, based on their efforts to tackle the literacy–technology interface in socioculturally informed ways.

Make strategic alignments—but of a different kind
School partnerships with outside organisations and groups are legion in the area of new technologies. Many are with software companies, retailers and other commercial organisations that help schools to acquire technology resources. For many schools this is a necessary strategy for meeting what they see as their resource needs, and we do not underestimate its role here.

We want to suggest another kind of strategic alignment—one that is linked to educational rather than infrastructural aspects of learning in the area of literacy and technology. It is a strategy whereby schools seek to build links with individuals, groups and organisations that can provide them with such things as access to sites of 'authentic' social practices using new technologies, to insider knowledge, and to opportunities to participate in 'mature' versions of Discourses. Partners can range from small and large businesses and service organisations to churches, clubs and community-based cultural workers. Learning opportunities can include spending time in sites of 'authentic' practice, as distinct from hit-and-run field trips, seeing first-hand how skills, concepts and activities engaged in class relate to 'real-life' practice and perhaps getting opportunities to participate in them. Learning opportunities may extend also to invitations to participate in joint projects or productions through outsourcing appropriate tasks to class groups, or to onsite participation in the company of 'experts'.

Access to insider knowledge can save schools a lot of time and money. It can provide reliable information about how to get maximum benefits for dollars spent, how to avoid expensive upgrades and unnecessary add-ons, and how to put allegedly 'obsolescent' equipment to productive ongoing use. Accessing insider knowledge replicates a principle presented at the beginning of this chapter: that the very process of learning how to identify high-quality strategic partners is itself an important educational process.

Ideas for professional development

Think beyond technology
It is important to avoid the trap of thinking that the main challenge presented by new technologies is to come to grips with them, particularly at the operational level of practice. To reassert points suggested above, we need to:

- think of both literacies and technologies as embedded in larger social practices and as related to each other in ways that are tied to the purposes, values, beliefs and identity-making aspects of these practices. Coming to understand what this means in theory and in practice is a crucial part of professional development.

- not learn 'technology' or 'literacy' in isolation from each other, or in decontextualised ways. Rather, we learn through participation in meaningful, social practices.

- develop our understanding of 'mature' forms of social practice as necessarily involving operational, cultural and critical dimensions.

- inform ourselves about 'authentic' forms of social practice that relate to the more specific learning requirements contained in curriculum statements, policies and syllabuses, so we can embed the more specific learnings in contexts of practice that are meaningful to students. This may involve forms of practice that are 'non-conventional' for education, such as elements of youth culture, leisure and recreation pursuits, as well as practices associated with life in the home where young people interact with a range of 'mature' uses of technologies and information with friends or by observing and interacting with older siblings and adults.

- know how to create learning activities that will connect in meaningful and motivating ways to what students are learning now with what they will do later in school and beyond school.

Engage in professional reading
The references we have used in this book provide clues to the kinds of texts we believe teachers will benefit from reading and studying. Many centre on sociocultural accounts of literacy, technology and learning, and involve a fair degree of formal theory and research.

We have tried to emphasise texts that are accessible, while at the same time theoretically sound. Of the other bodies of literature that are useful for teachers to sample in their efforts to inform their practice, we identify three types. (Some typical and readily available examples of each type are included in the appendix on p. 160.)

First, there is a literature relating to the question posed by Bill Green and Chris Bigum (1993) in their article 'Aliens in the classroom' (although, as the authors suggest, the aliens may well be teachers). They ask: Are there aliens in our classrooms and, if so, who are they? This seminal article highlights the importance for teachers of understanding contemporary forms of youth identities, commitments and involvements. (We hasten to add that certain texts we suggest may be borderline in taste for some readers. By the same token, good pedagogy begins with informed understanding of learners, including cultural knowledge of different kinds of youth identities.)

Second, we recommend delving into the burgeoning literature on issues associated with new technologies and social practices. After much initial hype about new communication and information technologies and their promise for social and personal progress, more critically informed and measured appraisals are appearing in accessible forms.

Finally, there are now many books dealing in diverse ways with social practices in cyberspace, emerging cultures associated with new technologies, and subcultures that interact with cultures connected to the use of new technologies. Such texts provide an excellent entrée to the cultural dimension of social practices. Although some of the practices are unacceptable from an educational standpoint, they provide valuable material for considering the operational, cultural and critical dimensions of practices involving new literacies and technologies. (As with some of those listed in the first section, several of these texts might be on the borders of good taste.)

Participate in collaborative projects

A useful form of professional development involves participating in collaborative projects at the literacy–technology interface based on sociocultural principles. Where communities of practice exist, an effective strategy is to involve participants at varying levels of expertise, so that those who are more 'novice' in one area can learn from others more 'expert', and vice versa: participants with expertise can contribute to the learning of others.

One such project is Literacy Web Australia (Schools on the

Web 1999). It contributes to the Schools on the Web project, where Microsoft, Optus Vision and Aussie Schoolhouse/Oz TeacherNet jointly host free web space for Australian P–12 schools. Any school with an internet connection and email account can register at the Schools on the Web site (1999). The idea behind the project began as a Special Program Schools Scheme (SPSS) bid for a share of funds, earmarked for schools working cooperatively on cluster projects. An original idea for a joint project, based on sharing best practice in literacy education with an emphasis on use of new technologies, between Abbotsdale and one other SPSS school in the region quickly escalated. Principals from all SPSS schools in the district met and decided they wanted their schools to join. At that point the focus of the project widened to include adding informative literacy articles and links to other sites. It seemed to the project director and others in the initial team that there was no point restricting the site to the participating schools. So the site expanded, issuing an invitation to submit case studies, and emerged as Literacy Web Australia.

The project aimed to provide opportunities for schools to:

- showcase best practice involving the intersection of literacy, new technologies and equity;
- provide a resource of theoretical knowledge in the form of up-to-date literacy articles;
- suggest links to other valuable literacy sites;
- encourage purposeful email communication between the schools in the cluster;
- give information about the SPSS scheme.

As an ongoing project, it builds on collaborative input from teachers, professional associations, researchers, academics, and anyone else with an interest in the topic. The Literacy Web index leads to five main webpages: Case Studies, Other Literacy Sites, SPSS Programs, Submit Your Project and Literacy Articles.

The links to 'Other Literacy Sites' and 'Literacy Articles' provide access to resources, many of which, especially the literacy articles, are steeped in a sociocultural perspective and present the work of some leading literacy researchers and scholars. But the real heart of the site involves the 'Case Studies'. Schools and teachers are invited to produce reports about learners' development of literacy and effective teaching and learning strategies based on their own experiences. The initial studies posted on the site involved participants from a cluster of schools working together on developing teaching and learning strategies for literacy education employing new technologies, peer tutoring and mentoring strategies, and informed use of scaffolding and structuring techniques based on a range of learning theories.

Projects currently published on the site include case studies of peer tutoring with a learning-disabled student, multimedia to present the history of a school, a peer reading project, an English as a second language (ESL) intervention using a small range of computer software, and a project which employs a range of technologies in literacy, numeracy and problem-solving activities and which includes a parent/family survey. Each case is cast in a teacher-researcher mould. They present the aims and purposes of the study, the theory and research that informs it, the study design, and the outcomes. Mentoring for teacher research can be pursued by following links, and their contacts, on Literacy Web Australia.

Total funding for the original project cluster was A$15 000 for each school to get a designated notebook computer, modem, internet connection and time, and a digital camera. Participants' experience in this project provides grassroots evidence for our belief that such web-based communities of practice offer readily available peer and expert assistance, built on goodwill and a shared sense of purpose. The project leader observed (email interview):

> All the schools learnt a lot about digital photography, file transfer and internet use in a purposeful context. [The project] provided a context to collect information about best practice and, perhaps, helped to generate best practice—in that schools had to look around at what was happening and start thinking about what was best practice in what they were doing and reflecting on.

Such projects offer facilities for self-initiated 'professional development by doing' with internet access and elementary knowledge of emailing. Collegial expertise becomes readily available from that point on. With direct links to professionally oriented sites and lists like Aussie SchoolHouse and Oz TeacherNet, Literacy Web Australia is a resource for eliciting and disseminating ideas and assistance relevant to most of the themes covered in this chapter. Here are some of the project leader's observations (email interview):

> I was surprised by the generosity of excellent authors/researchers contributing their work copyright-free for use on the site.
> Contacting and conversing with authors also led to great opportunities for me personally. For example, [one international

expert] engaged in a really interesting dialogue on equity issues with me, and now I'll meet with him in New York. I talked with [another US expert] who has now recommended me to [another US expert], and so now I'm speaking at the NY Educational Development Centre to share the equity in learning technologies work. I had communication with a journal editor that led to further publicity for the site in the 'Journal of Adolescent and Adult Education (JAAL)' [and the selection of Literacy Web Australia as JAAL Website of the Month]. Plus I ended up working with a school in Melbourne for a case study involving technology and ESL issues . . . Email communication generated by the site includes others apart from those involved in schools: for example, people involved in home schooling . . . who asked me to talk to their group about how computers can be used to benefit slow learners, as well as from other literacy organisations and individuals with questions about literacy or equity.

At a different level of initiative, professional associations provide a base from which relevant professional development activities can be launched. An example is the 'teachers first' project instigated by the Primary English Teaching Association of Australia (PETA): a mostly online, password-controlled, professional development program (PETA 1999).

Indeed, one useful school-based, professional development exercise would be to conduct online searches to locate internet-based sites and practices with the potential to support forms of self-initiated, professional development for individual teachers or groups of teachers along the lines we have advocated here. At the same time, we do well to remember what we have repeated many times: that professional development to enhance literacy education work at the interface with new technologies involves a good deal that has nothing to do with new technologies per se, and that 'technologies *support* learning and teaching, which always remains the main game' (Durrant & Green 1998: 11).

Principles for principals

The principal has a vital role to play in promoting and galvanising efforts by the school to make an educationally effective response to the literacy–technology challenge. Unless the principal assumes a key leadership role in mobilising and focusing staff to pursue an informed, coordinated and integrated approach to the literacy–technology interface, it is unrealistic to expect such an outcome to emerge.

We suggest that at least the following principles be adopted as guides to the principal's role. The principal should ensure that:

- school technology and literacy policies and programs are developed
  — in conjunction with each other,
  — with due reference to all learning areas,
  — with attention to issues of continuity, complementarity, workability and equity;
- integration of new technologies into classroom teaching and learning are tackled as a cross-curriculum initiative involving all members of staff;
- incentives are provided for teachers to develop effective links with other schools and community organisations, with a view to
  — sharing expertise and resources,
  — undertaking collaborative projects involving integration of new technologies into language and literacy learning;
- the school works in collaboration with its state/territory or sector administration and other sources of expertise to achieve an appropriate balance between investment in new technology infrastructure, operational and technical support, and teacher professional development;
- the school provides opportunities for parent and community members to participate in workshop activities involving new technologies.

FINAL REMARKS

Earlier, we cited the fifth principle of technorealism: Wiring the schools will not save them. In concluding our account, we draw readers' attention to the fourth principle of technorealism: Information is not knowledge. This principle is elaborated in the charter thus (Shenk 1998: 219–20):

> All around us information is moving faster and becoming cheaper to acquire, and the benefits are manifest. That said, the proliferation of data is also a serious challenge, requiring new measures of human discipline and scepticism. We must not confuse the thrill of acquiring or distributing information quickly with the more daunting task of converting it into knowledge and wisdom. Regardless of how advanced our computers become, we should

never use them as a substitute for our own [capacities] of awareness, perception, reasoning, and judgment.

The question of how schools and teachers can contribute to realising this principle is what this book has been largely about.

Appendix

TYPE 1: TEXTS THAT EMPHASISE LIFE AND PRACTICES IN AN ELECTRONIC WORLD

Bennahum, D. 1998 *Extra Life: Coming of Age in Cyberspace*, Basic Books, New York

Digitarts homepage 1999 June http://digitarts.va.com.au

GRRROWL 1999 June http://digitarts.va.com.au/frames.html, http://digitarts.va.com.au/grrrowl1

Howard, S. ed. 1997 *Wired Up: Young People and the Electronic Media*, Taylor & Francis, London

Howe, N. and Strauss, B. 1993 *13th Gen: Abort, Retry, Ignore, Fail?*, Vintage Books, New York

McCloud, S. 1994 *Understanding Comics*, Harper-Perennial, New York

Rushkoff, D. ed. 1994 *The GenX Reader*, Ballantine Books, New York

Rushkoff, D. 1996 *Playing the Future: How Kids' Culture Can Teach Us to Thrive in an Age of Chaos*, HarperCollins, New York:

Tunbridge, N. 1995 'The cyberspace cowboy' *Australian Personal Computer*, September

TYPE 2: TEXTS THAT FOCUS ON ISSUES ASSOCIATED WITH NEW TECHNOLOGIES

Shenk, D. 1998 *Data Smog*, HarperEdge, San Francisco

Franklin, U. 1990 *The Real World of Technology*, CBC Enterprises, Montreal

Grossman, W. 1997 *net.wars*, New York University Press, New York

Kling, R. ed. 1997 *Computerization and Controversy: Value Conflicts and Social Choices*, 2nd edn, Academic Press, San Diego

Loader, B. ed. 1998 *Cyberspace Divide*, Routledge, London

Robertson, H.-j. 1998 *No More Teachers, No More Books: The Commercialization of Canada's Schools*, McClelland & Stewart, Toronto

Roszak, T. 1994 *The Cult of Information*, University of California Press, Berkeley

Tenner, E. 1997 *Why Things Bite Back: Predicting the Problems of Progress*, Fourth Estate, London

Whitaker, R. 1999 *The End of Privacy: How Total Surveillance is Becoming a Reality*, The Free Press, New York

TYPE 3: TEXTS THAT DEAL WITH SOCIAL PRACTICES IN CYBERSPACE

Hafner, K. and Markoff, J. 1994 *Cyberpunk: Outlaws and Hackers on the Computer Frontier*, Ballantine Books, New York

Hafner, K. and Lyon, M. 1996 *Where Wizards Stay Up Late: The Origins of the Internet*, Touchstone Books, New York

Johnson, S. 1997 *Interface Culture: How New Technology Transforms the Way We Create and Communicate*, HarperEdge, San Francisco

Rushkoff, D. 1994 *Cyberia: Life in the Trenches of Hyperspace*, Harper, San Francisco

Rushkoff, D. 1996 *Media Virus: Hidden Agendas in Popular Culture*, 2nd edn, Ballantine Books, New York

Rushkoff, D. 1997 *Ecstacy Club: A Novel*, Riverhead Books, New York (contains language and ideas that could offend)

Stone, A. 1996 *The War of Desire and Technology at the Close of the Mechanical Age*, MIT Press, Cambridge, MA

References

Aronowitz, S. and Giroux, H. 1993 *Education Still Under Siege*, Bergin & Garvey, Westport, CT

Australian Education Council 1991 *Young People's Participation in Post-Compulsory Education and Training: Report of the Australian Education Council Review Committee*, Australian Government Publishing Service, Canberra

Becker, H.J. 1996 'How much will a truly empowering technology-rich education cost?' *Computerisation and Controversy: Value Conflicts and Social Choices*, 2nd edn, ed. R. Kling, Academic Press, San Diego, pp. 190–6

Bigum, C. 1997 'Teachers and computers: in control or being controlled' *Australian Journal of Education*, vol. 41, no. 3, pp. 247–61

Bigum, C. and Green, B. 1992 'Technologising literacy: the dark side of the dream' *Discourse: The Australian Journal of Educational Studies*, vol. 12, no. 2, pp. 4–28

——1995 *Managing Machines? Educational Administration and Information Technology*, Deakin University Press, Geelong, VIC

Bigum, C. and Kenway, J. 1998 'New information technologies and the ambiguous future of schooling—some possible scenarios' *International Handbook of Educational Change*, eds A. Hargreaves, M. Lieberman, M. Fullan and D. Hopkins, Kluwer Academic, Hingham, MA, pp. 375–95

Bloom, B.S. 1956 *Taxonomy of Educational Objectives: The Classification of Educational Goals*, David McKay, New York

Board of Studies, Victoria 1995 *Curriculum and Standards Framework: English*, Board of Studies, Carlton, VIC

——1997 *Information Technology in English: Using Information Technology to Help Students to Achieve the Learning Outcomes in the English Key Learning Area*, Board of Studies, Carlton, VIC

Boomer, G. 1988 'Reading the whole curriculum' *Metaphors and Meanings: Essays on English Teaching by Garth Boomer*, ed. B. Green, Australian Association for the Teaching of English, Adelaide

Bourdieu, P. 1977 'Cultural reproduction and social reproduction' *Power and Ideology in Education*, eds J. Karabel and A. Halsey, Oxford University Press, New York

Bruce, B. 1998 'New literacies' *Journal of Adult and Adolescent Literacy*, vol. 42, no. 1, pp. 46–9

Burbules, N. 1997 'Misinformation, malinformation, messed-up information, and mostly useless information: how to avoid getting tangled up in the "Net"' *Digital Rhetorics: Literacies and Technologies in Education—Current Practices and Future Directions*, vol. 3, ed. C. Lankshear et al., Department of Employment, Education, Training and Youth Affairs, Canberra, pp. 109–20

Christie, F., Devlin, B., Freebody, P., Luke, A., Threadgold, T. and Walton, C. 1991 *Teaching English Literacy: A Project of National Significance on the Pre-Service Preparation of Teachers for Teaching English Literacy, vol. 1*, Department of Employment, Education and Training, Canberra

Commonwealth of Australia 1994 *Creative Nation: Commonwealth Cultural Policy*, National Capital Printing, Canberra

Curriculum Corporation 1994a *A Statement on English for Australian Schools*, Curriculum Corporation, Carlton, VIC

——1994b *English—A Curriculum Profile for Australian Schools*, Curriculum Corporation, Carlton, VIC

——1994c *A Statement on Technology for Australian Schools*, Curriculum Corporation, Carlton, VIC

Delgado-Gaitan, C. 1990 *Literacy and Empowerment: The Role of Parents in Children's Education*, Falmer Press, London

Delpit, L. 1995 *Other People's Children: Cultural Conflict in the Classroom*, The New Press, New York

Department of Education, Employment Training and Youth Affairs (DEETYA) 1998 *Literacy for All: The Challenge for Australian Schools*, DEETYA, Canberra

Department of Education, Queensland 1994a *Principles of Effective Learning and Teaching*, Department of Education, Queensland, Brisbane

——1994b *English in Years 1 to 10 Queensland Syllabus Materials: English Syllabus for Years 1 to 10*, Department of Education, Queensland, Brisbane

——1994c *Literacy and Numeracy Strategy*, Department of Education, Queensland, Brisbane

——1994d *Shaping the Future: Review of the Queensland School Curriculum (The Wiltshire Report)*, 3 volumes, Department of Education, Queensland, Brisbane

——1994e *Shaping the Future: Summary of Recommendations*, Department of Education, Queensland, Brisbane

——1995a *Year 2 Diagnostic Net [Kit]*, Department of Education, Queensland, Brisbane

——1995b *Computers in Learning Policy*, Department of Education, Queensland, Brisbane

——1995c *Guidelines for the Use of Computers in Learning*, Department of Education, Queensland, Brisbane

Department of Education, Victoria 1998a *Learning Technologies in Victorian Schools 1998–2001*, Department of Education, Victoria, Melbourne

——1998b *Learning Technologies Teachers' Capabilities Statement* Department of Education, Victoria, Melbourne

——1999 http://www.sofweb.vic.edu.au [accessed June 1999]

Department of Employment, Education and Training (DEET) 1991a *Australia's Language: The Australian Language and Literacy Policy*, Australian Government Publishing Service, Canberra

——1991b *Australia's Language: The Australian Language and Literacy Policy*, Companion volume to the policy paper, Australian Government Publishing Service, Canberra

Digital Rhetorics 1999 http://www.business.cowan.edu.au/rhetorics/pdf_DL.htm [accessed June 1999]

Directorate of School Education, Victoria 1993 *Schools of the Future: Preliminary Paper*, Directorate of School Education, Melbourne

——1994 *Technologies for Enhanced Learning: Current and Future Use of Technologies in School Education. Government Working Party on the Use of Technology as an Education and Communication Facility in Schools*, Directorate of School Education, Melbourne

Drucker, P.F. 1993 *Post-Capitalist Society*, Harper, New York

Durrant, C. and Green, B. 1998 'Literacy and the New Technologies in School Education: Meeting the L(IT)eracy Challenge?', position paper for the NSW Department of Education and Training, NSW Department of Education and Training, Sydney

Education Queensland 1997 *Schooling 2001: School Kit 1997–1998*, Education Queensland, Brisbane

Franklin, U. 1990 *The Real World of Technology*, CBC Enterprises, Toronto

Freebody, P. 1992 'A socio-cultural approach: resourcing four roles as a literacy learner' *Prevention of Reading Failure*, eds A. Watson and A. Badenhop, Ashton Scholastic, Sydney, pp. 48–68

Freire, P. 1972 *Pedagogy of the Oppressed*, Penguin, Harmondsworth, England

Gardner, H. 1993 *Multiple Intelligences: The Theory in Practice*, Basic Books, New York

Gee, J.P. 1991 'What is literacy?' *Rewriting Literacy: Culture and the Discourse of the Other*, eds C. Mitchell and K. Weiler, Bergin & Garvey, New York, pp. 77–102

——1996 *Social Linguistics and Literacies*, 2nd edn, Falmer Press, London

——1997 'Foreword: a discourse approach to language and literacy' *Changing Literacies*, ed. C. Lankshear, Open University Press, Buckingham, pp. xiii–ix

Gee, J.P., Hull, G. and Lankshear, C. 1996 *The New Work Order: Behind the Language of the New Capitalism*, Allen & Unwin, Sydney

Green, B. 1988 'Subject-specific literacy and school learning: a focus on writing' *Australian Journal of Education*, vol. 32, no. 2, pp. 156–79

——1997a *Literacies and School Learning in New Times* paper presented at the Literacies in Practice: Progress and Possibilities Conference, South Australian Department of Education and Children's Services and the Catholic Education Office, Adelaide, 1 May

——1997b *Literacy, Information and the Learning Society*, paper presented at the Joint Conference of the Australian Association for the Teaching of English, the Australian Literacy Educators' Association and the Australian School Library Association, Darwin High School, Darwin, Northern Territory, 8–11 July

Green, B. and Bigum, C. 1993 'Aliens in the classroom' *Australian Journal of Education*, vol. 37, no. 2, pp. 119–41

——1996 'Hypermedia or media hype? New technologies and the future of literacy education' *The Literacy Lexicon*, eds G. Bull and M. Anstey, Prentice Hall, Sydney, pp. 193–204

——1998 'Re-tooling schooling? Information technology, cultural change and the future(s) of Australian education' *Schooling for a Fair Go*, eds J. Smyth, R. Hattam and M. Lawson, Federation Press, Sydney, pp. 71–96

Green, B., Hodgens, J. and Luke, A. 1994 *Debating Literacy in Australia: A Documentary History 1945–1994*, Australian Literacy Federation, Melbourne

Hafner, K. and Lyon, M. 1996 *Where Wizards Stay up Late: The Origins of the Internet*, Touchstone, New York

Heath, S.B. 1982 'What no bedtime story means: narrative skills at home and school' *Language and Society*, vol. 11, pp. 49–76

——1983 *Ways with Words: Language, Life, and Work in Communities and Schools*, Cambridge University Press, Cambridge

Heath, S.B. and McLaughlin, M. 1994 'Learning for anything everyday' *Journal of Curriculum Studies*, vol. 26, no. 5, pp. 471–89

Heath, S.B. and Mangiola, L. 1991 *Children of Promise: Literate Activity in Linguistically and Culturally Diverse Classrooms*, National Education Association of the United States, Washington, DC

Hodas, S. 1996 'Technology refusal and the organisational culture of schools' *Computerisation and Controversy: Value Conflicts and Social Choices*, 2nd edn, ed. R. Kling, Academic Press, San Diego, pp. 197–218

Idhe, D. 1990 *Technology and the Lifeworld: From Garden to Earth*, Penguin, Harmondsworth, England

Jones, A. 1986 At school I've got a chance: ideology and social reproduction in a secondary school, unpublished PhD, University of Auckland, Auckland

Kliebard, H.M. 1992 'Vocational education as symbolic action: connecting schooling with the workplace' *Forging the American Curriculum: Essays in Curriculum History and Theory*, Routledge, New York

Knobel, M. 1999 *Everyday Literacies: Students, Discourses and Social Practice*, Peter Lang, New York

Knobel, M. and Lankshear, C. 1997 *Ways with Windows: What Different People Do with the Same Equipment*, paper presented at the Language, Learning and

Culture: Unsettling Certainties Joint National Conference of the AATE, ALEA and ASLA, Darwin, 8–11 July

Kress, G. 1995 *Writing the Future: English and the Making of a Culture of Innovation*, National Association for the Teaching of English, Sheffield

Lankshear, C. 1997 *Changing Literacies*, Open University Press, Buckingham

——1998 'Frameworks and workframes: literacy policies and new orders' *Unicorn*, vol. 24, no. 2, pp. 43–58

Lankshear, C. and Bigum, C. in press 'Literacies and new technologies in school settings' *Journal of Curriculum Studies*

Lankshear, C., Bigum, C., Durrant, C., Green, B., Honan, E., Morgan, W., Murray, J., Snyder, I. and Wild, M. 1997 *Digital Rhetorics: Literacies and Technologies in Education—Current Practices and Future Directions*, Department of Employment, Education, Training and Youth Affairs, Canberra

Lave, J. and Wenger, E. 1991 *Situated Learning: Legitimate Peripheral Participation*, Cambridge University Press, Cambridge

Lemke, J.L. 1995 *Textual Politics: Discourse and Social Dynamics*, Taylor & Francis, London

Lo Bianco, J. and Freebody, P. 1997 *Australian Literacies: Informing National Policy on Literacy Education*, Language Australia: National Languages and Literacy Institute of Australia, Canberra

Marvin, C. 1988 *When Old Technologies were New: Thinking about Communications in the Late Nineteenth Century*, Oxford University Press, New York

Michaels, S. 1986 'Narrative presentations: an oral preparation for literacy with first graders' *The Social Construction of Literacy*, ed. J. Cook-Gumperz, Cambridge University Press, Cambridge, pp. 94–116

Ministry of Education, Victoria 1986 *English and Computers, P–12: Recommendations for the Use of Computers in English and English as a Second Language for Years P–12*, Schools Division, Ministry of Education, Melbourne

——1988 *English Language Framework: P–10*, Schools Division, Ministry of Education, Melbourne

Moll, L. 1992 'Literacy research in community and classrooms: sociocultural approach' *Multidisciplinary Perspectives on Literacy Research*, eds R. Beach, J. Green, M. Kamil and T. Shanahan, National Council for Research in Education and National Council for the Teaching of English, Urbana, IL, pp. 211–44

Morgan, R. 1996 'Pantextualism, everyday life and media education' *Discourse: The Australian Journal of Educational Studies*, vol. 16, no. 1, pp. 14–34

National Board of Employment Education and Training (NBEET) 1995 *Converging Technology, Work and Learning*, National Board of Employment, Education and Training, Canberra

Negroponte, N. 1996 *Being Digital*, Hodder Headline Australia, Sydney

Pacey, A. 1983 *The Culture of Technology*, 1st edn, Basil Blackwell, Oxford

Papert, S. 1993 *The Children's Machine: Rethinking School in the Age of the Computer*, Basic Books, New York

Parliament of Commonwealth of Australia 1991 *Australia as an Information Society:*

Grasping New Paradigms, Australian Government Publishing Services, Canberra

——1992 *The Literacy Challenge: A Report on Strategies for Early Intervention for Literacy and Learning for Australian Children*, House of Representatives Standing Committee on Employment, Education and Training, Australian Government Publishing Service, Canberra

Peters, M. and Lankshear, C. 1996 'Critical literacy and digital texts' *Educational Theory*, vol. 46, no. 1, pp. 51–70

Poster, M. 1990 *The Mode of Information: Poststructuralism and Social Context*, Polity Press, Cambridge

Postman, N. 1996 'Virtual students, digital classrooms' *Minutes of the Lead Pencil Club*, ed. B. Henderson, Pushcart Press, New York, pp. 197–215

Primary English Teachers Association of Australia (PETA) 1999 http://www.peta.edu.au [accessed June 1999]

Reich, R. 1992 *The Work of Nations: Preparing Ourselves for 21st Century Capitalism*, Vintage Books, New York

Reid, J.-A. 1997 'Generic practice' *Australian Journal of Language and Literacy*, vol. 20, no. 2, pp. 148–55

Robertson, H.-j. 1998 *No More Teachers, No More Books: The Commercialization of Canada's Schools*, McClelland & Stewart, Toronto

Rogoff, B. 1984 'Introduction: thinking and learning in social context' *Everyday Cognition: Cognitive Development in a Social Context*, eds B. Rogoff and J. Lave, Harvard University Press, Cambridge, MA, pp. 1–8

——1990 *Apprenticeship in Thinking: Cognitive Development in a Social Context*, Oxford University Press, New York

——1995 'Observing sociocultural activity on three planes: participatory appropriation, guided participation, apprenticeship' *Sociocultural Studies of Mind*, eds J. Wertsch, P. del Rio and A. Alvarez, Cambridge University Press, New York, pp. 139–64

Roszak, T. 1996 'Dumbing us down' *New Internationalist*, December, vol. 286

Schools on the Web 1999 http://www.schools.ash.org.au [accessed June 1999]

Secada, W.G. 1989 'Educational equity versus equality of education: an alternative conception' *Equity in Education*, ed. W.G. Secada, Falmer Press, New York, pp. 68–88

Shenk, D. 1998 *Data Smog*, revd/updated edn, HarperEdge, San Francisco

Smith, F. 1985 'A metaphor for literacy: creating worlds or shunting information?' *Language, Literacy and Learning: The Nature and Consequences of Reading and Writing*, eds D. Olson, N. Torrance and A. Hildyard, Cambridge University Press, Cambridge, pp. 195–213

Snyder, I. 1996 *Hypertext: The Electronic Labyrinth*, Melbourne University Press, Melbourne

——ed. 1997 *Page to Screen: Taking Literacy into the Electronic Era*, Allen & Unwin, Sydney/Routledge, London

——in press 'Technology rhetorics: taking a critical perspective' *Text Technology*

Sproull, L. and Kiesler, S. 1991 *Connections: New Ways of Working in the Networked Organisation*, MIT Press, Cambridge, MA

Stewart-Dore, N. 1996 'Confronting a cause celebre: how might we raise a literacy teacher's profile?' *Language Learning: Secondary Thoughts*, vol. 4, no. 1, pp. 8–22

Street, B.V. 1984 *Literacy in Theory and Practice*, Cambridge University Press, Cambridge

Taylor, S., Rizvi, F., Lingard, B. and Henry, M. 1997 *Educational Policy and the Politics of Change*, Routledge, London

Tinkler, D., Lepani, B. and Mitchell, J. 1996. *Education and Technology Convergence: A Survey of Technological Infrastructure in Education and the Professional Development and Support of Educators and Trainers in Information and Communication Technologies*, Commissioned Report 43, Australian Government Publishing Service, Canberra

Tuman, M. 1992 *Word Perfect: Literacy in the Computer Age*, Falmer Press, London

Turkle, S. 1995 *Life on the Screen: Identity in the Age of the Internet*, Simon & Schuster, New York

US Department of Education 1996 *Getting America's Students Ready for the 21st Century: Meeting the Technology Literacy Challenge*, Report to the nation on technology and education, US Department of Education, Washington, DC

Vygotsky, L. 1962 *Thought and Language*, trans. E. Hanfmann and G. Vakar, MIT Press, Cambridge, MA

Waldrop, M.M. 1992 *Complexity: The Emerging Science at the Edge of Chaos and Order*, Viking, London

Winters, K. 1996 *America's Technology Literacy Challenge*, US Department of Education, Office of the Under Secretary k.winters@inet.ed.gov [posted 17 February 1996 acwl@unicorn.acs.ttu.edu]

Winton, T. 1993. *Lockie Leonard, Human Torpedo*, Penguin, Melbourne

Index

References to figures are in **bold**

incidental learning about genres, 79
indoctrination *see* socialisation
information
    complementary skills in, 123–4
    distinct from knowledge, 158–9
    equity of access to, 57–8
    no longer subordinate to text,
        39–40
information literacy *see* literacy
information technology *see*
    technology
Information Technology in English (Vic),
    70
in-service programs *see* teacher
    training
insiders, 139–43
    consultation with, 152–3
    teachers' need to be, 37
    viewpoints of, 146
interest groups in policy making, 50–1
Internet access
    adapts to classroom
        environment, 117–18
    at Tipping Primary, 89–91
    books about, 154
    complementarity in, 123
    critical attitudes to, 35–6
    cultural context of, 33
    effect on classroom culture, 112
    fragility of, 8, 16, 114
    maximising, 6
    not a panacea, 147–8
    role in literacy, 41–2
    skills in, 149–50
    to overseas schools, 113
    to teaching resources, 71
    via Optus Vision, 11
inventions, class project work on,
    84–5

Janine (case study teacher), 103–4
John (case study teacher), 97–9
journalism, social practice of, 104–5

Kate (case study teacher), 98–101
Kenway, J., xvi, xviii, 121
Key Learning Areas
    expertise of teachers, 144
    in National Curriculum project, 62
    little consultation between, 74

KidPix Studio (software), 98–100
Kiesler, S., 36
KLAs *see* Key Learning Areas
knowledge, distinct from
    information, 158–9

language
    used in a Discourse, 29
    used in policy making, 55
language backgrounds other than
    English *see* non-English
    background students
language learning, 78–9
laptop computers
    available to students, 11
    unnecessary use of, 105
Lave, J., 42
leadership
    commitment to outside expertise,
        135
    in changing school culture, 20–1
    national policy on, 59
    principles for, 157–8
learning
    about technology skills, 2, 122
    ambiguity of term, 60–61
    defined, 65
    goals of, 143
    principles of, 64–5
    sociocultural perspective on, 42–4
    traditional approaches to, 22
    vs acquisition, 43
learning activities
    at Abbotsdale Primary, 78
    attempts to make 'real', 118
    international scope of, 113
    rotation in, 84–5
*Learning Technologies in Victorian Schools
    1998–2001*, 50
*Learning Technologies Teachers'
    Capabilities Statement*, 71
learning technology advisers, 88–9
Lemke, J.L., 32, 38
liberal humanist tradition, 39–40
librarians
    as facilitators of Internet access,
        11
    in curriculum design, 77–8
    national policy on, 59
life trajectories, 44, 129–31